25 ROLE PLAYS FOR DEVELOPING COUNSELLING SKILLS

25 ROLE PLAYS FOR DEVELOPING COUNSELLING SKILLS

David Couper and Jacqueline Stewart

Gower

First published 1993 by Gower Publishing

This paperback edition published 1995 by
Gower Publishing
Gower House
Croft Road
Aldershot
Hants GU11 3HR
England

Gower
Old Post Road
Brookfield
Vermont 05036
USA

CIP catalogue records for this book are available from the British Library

ISBN 0-566-07663-2

Printed in Great Britain by Antony Rowe Ltd, Chippenham, Wiltshire.
Typeset in 12pt Century Old Style by Poole Typesetting (Wessex) Ltd, Bournemouth, Dorset.

Contents

Preface

In creating these role plays we have tried to provide a realistic framework within which participants will be able to practise their counselling skills. The 'counsellors' should always be themselves, using the information provided as a basis for modelling the counselling process. Only the 'counsellees' need to actually play a role.

Both of us have experience of counselling within voluntary organizations, as well as in the workplace, and we have drawn directly from our own experiences to build these role plays. Truth can definitely be stranger than fiction!

David Couper
Jacqueline Stewart

Introduction

This manual contains 25 role plays for use in counselling at work. They vary in content but all have the same aim of giving participants an opportunity to act out , in a non-threatening, authentic setting, a counsellor role which they could encounter in their working life.

The role plays enable the trainer to:

- see how a participant acts and behaves when faced with certain events or factors;
- see what weaknesses and fears or strengths and qualities a participant brings to a problem;
- allow practice of training content studied during the training period;
- explore situations practically in a training room instead of on the job;
- train in a risk-free environment.

Role plays can be used in a number of ways. We have set out four alternative methods, although there may be others which you prefer to use. The role plays are designed as materials and aids for your training events, not methodologies or prescriptions for the style of training.

The role plays in this book are concerned with counselling at work. They cover a range of topics, some directly related to work issues, such as teambuilding, and some indirectly related, such as employees and alcohol. Some of the topics require the participants to use their own knowledge and fears about particular circumstances. Others provide complete worlds. Those which ask the participant to use their own knowledge and feelings help to pinpoint problems in the participants themselves. This can be very useful if problems are suspected, as the role plays can help participants to share difficult feelings without being made to feel awkward. If sensible guidelines are followed, there is little risk of creating more problems or making the problems worse for the counsellee, and so participants are likely to take chances and experiment. Those role plays where the world has been defined enable the participants to practise their counselling skills even if they have no experience of the actual problems presented.

With two exceptions the exercises have been designed so that participants of either sex can play all the roles. Only in the role plays featuring sexist behaviour have the relevant genders been specified.

We have set the role plays in a variety of industries, companies and organizations. However, it will be clear that the point of the role play is not to discuss any particular type of business but to practise counselling techniques, so don't be put off if the role play you choose is set in a different sphere of work from your own.

The benefits of counselling may be summarized as follows:

- For the counsellee: gives greater understanding of their own performance and enables them to improve.
- For the counsellor: improves understanding of their role in the counsellee's own development, thus increasing job satisfaction and self-esteem.
- For the organization: better individual performance means better teamwork and an overall improvement.

THE NATURE OF COUNSELLING

There are various styles of counselling but the role plays in this volume are for PERFORMANCE COUNSELLING, not for THERAPY COUNSELLING. The aim is to help the counsellee to know and 'own' his/her performance strengths and weaknesses, not help him/her to work through deep psychological problems.

Every manager or supervisor has a responsibility to counsel staff, and to guide and direct employees in their daily work. Members of staff need to be told how they are performing, whether they are meeting standards and how they can improve. Often it is only through counselling that these improvements can take place.

An employee who is late or who is producing careless work may be suffering from the effects of bereavement or alcohol. Dealing with the staff member without counselling them to find out if there is a particular cause of the behaviour will probably not help. Counselling a worker may reveal that there is a drink problem, and although this offers no solution, it does enable help and advice to be aimed in the right direction. The employee has to take responsibility for his/her own life and drinking problems but the manager can advise and support throughout this period.

THE COUNSELLING INTERVIEW

Here is a three-part model for conducting a counselling interview.

Before

- Collect and digest all relevant information.
- Research any specialist help you may want to offer – telephone number of AA, contact in Personnel Department and so on.
- Decide on relevant approach for counsellee.
- Choose an appropriate time.
- Arrange for a quiet place, with no interruptions.
- Identify your support. Counselling can produce bad feelings within you which need to be talked about.

During

Opening

- Try to put the counsellee at ease.
- If possible establish a rapport, perhaps by talking about a subject not related to the interview but of interest to both of you – the new social club, or the squash ladder.
- State the purpose of the interview.

Analyse the situation

- Establish the problem carefully in non-judgemental terms, e.g. 'I've noticed you've been late'.
- Then allow the counsellee to talk. You should:
  - listen
  - clarify
  - keep silent
  - examine the problem thoroughly
  - keep calm even if the counsellee becomes angry or upset
  - summarize.
- Enable the counsellee to state their problems.
- Allow them to trust you by giving them time and space to talk.
- Highlight positive elements which have been mentioned by the counsellee.
- Suggest other positive elements but be prepared for them to be rejected.

Discuss solutions

Once the situation is clear the counsellee should be encouraged to think of solutions. Do not try to improse a solution – it will probably be rejected. Instead, suggest alternatives with the possible pros and cons but do not recommend. The counsellee needs to own the problem and be responsible for deciding on the solution.

Make a contract

Whether the counsellee decides on a solution or only recognizes the problem, you should aim to make some kind of contract. This could be an appointment with a specialist, e.g. a debt counsellor, or an agreement that the counsellee will be honest about his/her feelings in the future and feel free to talk about them. In return promise practical help, support, advice or time to listen, depending on need. An action plan may be appropriate.

After

- Summarize the situation, the solutions and the contract.
- Assess yourself. You may have become involved in some of the counsellee's problems. You need some support so that you can talk this through.
- Plan your follow-up.
- Carry out any promises of practical help, e.g. talking to line manager.

There are other models which you may feel more comfortable with. The role plays can be used with different counselling styles and models. They are designed to be used flexibly, to be interesting and motivating for participants and a useful tool in your trainer's repertoire.

The next section outlines some different ways of using the role plays.

How to use the role plays

Many trainers have their own preferred ways of conducting role plays, depending on their ideology, the objectives, the participants and even the equipment and time available. In order to avoid implying that each of these 25 role plays has a specific method, we set out below four different methods to choose from. Each one mentions not only the method but also the relevant effect on numbers of participants, equipment, timing and the quantity of documents to be photocopied.

These four methods are not exclusive. Should you feel that you prefer to use another approach, you still have the role play documents to work with.

METHOD 1 – USING CCTV

Background

This method is most appropriate when all the participants need to be able to see and hear themselves conducting a counselling session. The TV recordings can then be used to give praise where due and therefore raise confidence. An added benefit is that the counsellor will usually identify his/her own mistakes very readily which leads the way to future improvements in performance. The instructions below provide for half the group to role-play the counsellor. To give everyone a chance, take a second role play and repeat the procedure with allocated roles reversed.

Group size

12 participants working in pairs.

Suggested timing

- 15 minutes' preparation.
- 15–20 minutes for recording each role play.
- 15–20 minutes to review and give feedback on each recording.
- 15 minutes for a final debriefing.

This makes a total of approximately 3½ hours.

Materials required

- 6 copies each of the counsellor and counsellee documents.
- 12 copies of any background information sheets.
- 12 copies of the Observer's Form for everyone to use during the review and feedback sessions.
- Video camera, TV monitor, VCR and 6 video tapes.
- Separate room for recording.
- Flipchart and pens.

Method

1. Divide participants into pairs and allocate one person in each pair the role of the counsellor and the other the role of counsellee.
2. Distribute copies of the relevant roles and any background information sheets.
3. Allow 15–20 minutes for preparation and emphasize that counsellors should just be themselves and apply their counselling skills to the situation presented to them. Ask counsellees to role-play their situation with as much feeling as possible. If they find this difficult, ask them to imagine what it might be like or relate to their own or friends' experiences.
4. Draw up an order for the role plays, either by asking for the pairs to volunteer or by having a raffle. Write up the order on the flip chart.
5. Take the first pair into the syndicate room where the video equipment has been set up, focused on the table and chairs where the session will take place. Explain that they will have 15–20 minutes to conduct the interview. You can give them updates on how the time is going.
6. Put a tape into the VCR or the camcorder and start the recording. At this point you may either stay in the room as an observer, or leave them alone and return to the main conference room where the others are still preparing for their turn.

7. After each pair has finished put a new tape into the machine before another pair begins.
8. When all sessions have been recorded, get the whole group together to watch the videos. Distribute copies of the Observer's Form and use that as a basis for the discussion of each role play.
9. For the debriefing, refer to that section of the specific role play you are using.

Additional guidance

If you choose to remain in the room while the counselling session is going on, make notes of any points of interest to raise with the whole group afterwards. If it is possible to make a note from the counter on the VCR, you can fast-forward the tape to the exact place you wish to highlight. Otherwise, just show some excerpts from the tape. If you only have 2 or 3 role plays to review, your time may allow for more in-depth feedback. Give each participant the video tape of their session so they can review it later in full.

METHOD 2 – TRAINER AS OBSERVER

Background

This method is ideal when someone has asked for or been offered the opportunity to examine their counselling skills as opposed to attending a course. As this method has just one counselling pair working with the trainer, it is possible to go into much more depth than when a whole group is present.

Group size

2 participants.

Suggested timing

- 15 minutes' preparation.
- 15–20 minutes for the role play.
- 30 minutes for the feedback and debriefing.

This makes a total of approximately 1 hour.

Materials required

- 1 copy each of the counsellor and counsellee role play documents plus any background information.
- 1 copy of the Observer's Form for yourself.

Method

1. Give each participant their role play document and any background information.
2. Allow 15 minutes to prepare. Remind the counsellor to be him/herself and the counsellee to role-play with as much feeling as possible. If they find this difficult, see if they can relate to any similar personal experience or that of their friends.
3. Explain that when the role play starts you will sit quietly in the corner of the room, listening and observing what happens in order to comment later.
4. Ask the participants to sit at the place prepared for them and to begin.
5. Use the Observer's Form to make notes during the role play and keep the participants informed of any time pressures.
6. When they have finished, follow the instructions for the debriefing contained in that section of the specific role play.

Additional guidance

As no-one else is present during this method, it is possible to concentrate on the counselling techniques of the individual concerned. Even so, care must be taken to ensure that all comments are constructive. If necessary, elements of the role play can be re-enacted to practise new approaches or phrases deemed preferable.

METHOD 3 – GROUP AS OBSERVERS

Background

This method is useful when time is limited and when the course objectives do not require all participants to demonstrate their counselling skills. Just one pair acting out the role play in front of everyone else becomes the subject for discussion and is a memorable conclusion to a session. Care needs to be taken when choosing the pair to do the role play. After all, they will be 'on stage' in front of their colleagues. So, either ask for volunteers or choose participants you have confidence in.

Group size

12 participants

Suggested timing

- 15 minutes for preparation.
- 15–20 minutes for the role play.
- 30 minutes for the feedback and debriefing.

This makes a total of approximately 1 hour.

Materials required

- 11 copies of the counsellor role play document.
- 11 copies of the counsellee role play document.
- 12 copies of any background information documents.
- 11 copies of the Observer's Form.

Method

1. Decide who is going to provide the demonstration of counselling skills and give them their role play documents.
2. Give the rest of the participants copies of both sides of the role play situation and any background information so they can study it.
3. Allocate 15 minutes for preparation.
4. Ask the counsellor and the counsellee to come out to the front and arrange their seating in full view of the rest of the group.
5. Ask the others to listen and observe the counselling session, making notes on the Observer's Form to discuss later. On no account are they to interrupt.

6. When the role play is over, conduct the feedback and debriefing according to the instructions on the specific role play.

METHOD 4 – GROUPS OF 3

Background

This method has the participants working in groups of three where one person takes the role of counsellor, another the role of counsellee and the third acts as the observer. In this way, all of the role plays can take place simultaneously, with you as an itinerant observer. Only one-third of the participants explore their counselling skills; therefore it may be useful to repeat the procedure after reallocating the roles within each group. If the particular role play involves the uncovering of previously unknown facts it would be best to distribute a new role play situation each time.

Group size

12 participants working in 4 groups of 3.

Suggested timing

- 15 minutes' preparation.
- 15–20 minutes for the role play.
- 10 minutes for feedback within the counselling groups of 3.
- 20 minutes for a debriefing with the whole group together.

This makes a total of approximately 1 hour.

Materials required

- 4 copies each of the counsellor and counsellee's documents and observer form.
- 4 syndicate rooms.

Method

1. Divide the participants into groups of 3 and within those, allocate the roles of counsellor, counsellee and observer.
2. Distribute the relevant documents to each person for their role.

3. Allow 15 minutes for preparation.
4. Tell each counselling group where their syndicate room is. Explain that you will come into the rooms from time to time just to observe a little of what is going on. You will not interrupt them and they must continue with the session.
5. Instruct the counselling groups to have a private feedback session when their 20 minutes is up. The counsellor should be asked to comment first, then the counsellee and finally the observer who must then report back to the whole group.
6. Call all the counselling groups back together and debrief according to the instructions for the specific role play.

Using the observer's form

The observer's form is designed to be used during role plays either by the trainer, the appointed observer or both, depending on the method chosen. The observer should be briefed to sit at a discreet distance from the role play and not become involved in any way. He/she should concentrate on listening and observing how the counselling interview progresses.

The form contains six boxes with headings from 'Greetings' down to 'Solutions' in which the observer should note down how the counsellor and the counsellee handle each aspect of the interview. For example, under 'Body language', it might be noted that the counsellee didn't make eye contact with the counsellor until asked '. . . . . .'. The observer should then use the notes made on the form to add to the discussion during the debriefing. However, if you are using a different model for the counselling process you may wish to adapt the Observer's Form accordingly.

OBSERVER'S FORM

	Counsellor	Counsellee
Greetings		
Opening		
Questions		
Listening		
Body language		
Solutions		

Using the action plan

A copy of the personal action plan should be handed out to each participant at the end of the debriefing session. Ask them to note down those aspects of their counselling style or behaviours which they intend to work on over the next few months. These points should be based on their own experience in the role play and/or from the feedback they have received afterwards. Advise them to review their action plan at their chosen date with another participant, manager or trainer, to reinforce the learning which has taken place.

ACTION PLAN

Action	By: Date	Discussed with	Comments

Symbols

Trainer's guide

Handout

THE ROLE PLAYS

Tg

1

All work and no play

Aims

To provide the opportunity for a counselling session with anyone, be they subordinate, colleague or superior, whom you identify as a workaholic.

Materials required

- Document 1.1 – Brief for counsellor
- Document 1.2 – Brief for counsellee
- Observer's Form
- Personal Action Plan

Background

Being a workaholic has a variety of origins. We may be genetically programmed that way, it may be a habit acquired at school or college with the encouragement and praise of parents and teachers, or it may be a gradual result of working in an organization where everyone is expected to devote themselves, both in and out of normal working hours, to getting the work done.

Whatever the origins, being a workaholic is something which others are likely to notice before we realize it ourselves. The best chance of a cure comes when an individual accepts and recognizes they have a problem, as they are then motivated to take remedial action. This role play provides an opportunity to raise the topic with an apparent sufferer and help them find some solutions.

Method

Chose one of the four methods described in the Introduction. Prepare copies of the relevant documents and brief the participants accordingly.

Debriefing

1. Bring all the counselling groups back together and ask the counsellors to comment on their own use of counselling skills. What did they do well, what do they wish they hadn't said and what did they learn from it?
2. Ask the counsellees to describe how it felt to them. Were they presented with a *fait accompli*, were they 'accused', were they given practical advice and did they feel able to explore their own feelings?
3. Ask the observers for any comments they can add to the discussion.
4. Relate what has happened to any model of counselling you are using on your course.
5. Handout out Personal Action Plans for completion.

BRIEF FOR COUNSELLOR

You have noticed lately that a colleague/boss/subordinate has been exhibiting many of the symptoms of workaholism, for example:

- Coming in early and staying very late without appearing to get more done.
- Giving people work at the last minute and expecting them to meet unreasonably tight deadlines.
- Setting unobtainable objectives for themselves and others.
- Looking tired and drawn and losing weight.
- Eating too much junk food and putting on weight.
- Desk in such a mess that no-one can find anything.
- Always rushing from one meeting to another.
- Never having time for people.
- Always taking work home.

You feel that at best they are suffering from stress and at worst they are heading for a breakdown in their personal relationships or maybe a heart attack. This person doesn't take criticism well and you know it won't be easy, but you feel it is your duty as a colleague to offer a helping hand.

Prepare for the meeting you have asked them to.

BRIEF FOR COUNSELLEE

Your boss/colleague/subordinate has asked you into their office for a private meeting. You are not only puzzled; you are angry because you have many deadlines to meet this week and every minute counts.

With the pressure from your boss and the new mortgage to worry about, you can't afford not to perform well. Your partner has been complaining recently that you either work late or bring work home. You can't see what all the fuss is about: this is your contribution to your joint future and if you don't work hard and get promotion now, opportunities might pass you by.

Everyone in the office seems to have become a little slow of late and you are aware you have been a bit short-tempered with some people. Is this why you are going to this meeting?

Prepare yourself.

2

Career crossroads

Aim

To help managers counsel employees whose appraisal has shown they have reached the end of their career development within the organization.

Materials required

- Document 2.1 – Brief for manager
- Document 2.2 – Brief for employee
- Observer's Form
- Personal Action Plan

Background

Annual appraisals have many potential outcomes: employee continues as usual, employee asks for or is sent on a training course, there is a pay rise, new objectives are set, procedural changes are agreed, employee feels either motivated or dissatisfied and so on. However, from time to time, an honest appraisal interview can highlight the fact that this person has really achieved everything they can in this job and there are no new challenges to meet within it. In that case, the idea of moving on to another department or to another organization has to be dealt with. Such a solution would also mean a successor being chosen and trained for the job. This role play allows the participants to explore ways of handling such an interview.

Method

Choose one of the four methods described in the Introduction. Prepare copies of the relevant documents and brief the participants accordingly.

Debriefing

1. Ask managers how they felt. What options did they consider and what additional information do they need for the future?
2. Ask the counsellees how they felt. Were they listened to? Did they learn anything useful and did they feel valued by the manager?
3. Ask the observers for any additional comments.
4. Summarize with reference to the counselling model you are using.
5. Hand out Personal Action Plans for completion.

Additional guidance

One options is for an employee in these circumstances to start their own business. If this is a possibility, it would be useful to get details of courses run by local colleges to help people start a business.

If retraining is available within the organization, the National Training Index provides details of most courses on offer in the UK.

BRIEF FOR MANAGER

You are reaching the end of an appraisal interview with a trusted and valued member of your team. Over the years this person has faced, tackled and succeeded with all the changes of company policy, changes of ownership and changes in technology. At the moment there seem to be no new challenges on the horizon. As your interview so far has shown, this person is now coasting along in neutral, feeling bored and merely getting the job done.

You can understand this, but as you have no intention of retiring yourself there is obviously no immediate opportunity for promotion. So, the question is, what do you do about a member of staff whose lack of motivation could rub off on the others and eat away at your hard-earned team spirit?

The dilemma is that you don't want to lose them but you can't risk the effects of keeping them. You now need to find out exactly how this person feels, how they see their own future developing and help them forward from there.

Prepare for the interview.

BRIEF FOR EMPLOYEE

You are in an appraisal interview with your boss. For the first time for years, it seems that your work has only just been satisfactory and if you are honest it is because you are getting bored. In the past there always seemed to be changes taking place. There were takeovers to contend with and the subsequent changes of policy and the installation and updating of new technology.

Things have become very static and you feel no sense of danger or challenge any more. You wouldn't mind promotion, for example, but you don't know what the boss's plans are. You hate to admit it, but this may be the moment to make a really big step into the unknown. Your mortgage payments aren't too steep any more and the children are all away earning their own living, but still it is hard to think of letting the company down.

You feel that it is at least worth discussing your feelings with the boss and getting some feedback on your supposed options of waiting for promotion or launching into a self-employed status to use your technological skills with companies who don't have their own qualified staff. Your main fear would be lack of knowledge of how to run a small company, especially things like accounts and VAT.

Prepare for the interview.

3

Correct business dress

Aim

To provide an opportunity to handle the sensitive issue of personal dress code with an employee.

Materials required

- Document 3.1 – Brief for manager
- Document 3.2 – Brief for graduate
- Observer's Form
- Personal Action Plan

Background

Dress is a very personal question which often bears no relation to the person's ability to carry out their job satisfactorily. Nevertheless, many organizations have an unwritten code that prescribes what is acceptable and what is not. Where safety is concerned there will be formal regulations covering protective clothing such as goggles, gloves, overalls, hard-toe shoes etc.

Most people subconsciously absorb the prevailing norm of dress and adapt their own style to it. Others, however, ignore the signals around them and come to work dressed inappropriately for the environment in order to maintain what they see as their right to individuality or maybe to show they don't care about such things. If someone is allowed to continue in this way, others can start to feel aggrieved because they might like to be more adventurous with their clothes but had been prepared to accept the status quo until this person came along and challenged it.

A manager has a duty at least to make the individual aware of the organization's expectations and/or rules and make it clear what, if any, long-term effects dress might have on career prospects.

Method

Choose one of the four methods described in the Introduction. Prepare copies of the relevant documents and brief the participants accordingly.

Debriefing

1. Ask the managers how they felt about this interview. How difficult was it to raise the subject? Were they happy with the outcome?
2. Ask the counsellees how they felt they were treated by the managers. Did they understand the point – would they in fact agree to make some adjustments?
3. Ask the observers, if used, for any additional comments they may have, especially if there was any illuminating body language.
4. Relate the outcomes back to your model for counselling skills.
5. Hand out copies of the Personal Action Plan for completion.

BRIEF FOR MANAGER

You feel very awkward about this. On your staff is a graduate trainee who started a couple of months ago. Intellectual ability is not in any doubt as he/she obtained a first class degree in Economics from an Oxbridge University, and your boss has made it clear that the organization is delighted to have attracted such a high calibre mind.

However, although you appreciate that it takes some time for students to make the transition to the working environment, you are concerned about what might seem a superficial problem – clothing. He/she arrives every morning in exactly the same clothes. Shoes are never cleaned and look as if they need repairing. The same old sweatshirt with holes at the elbow seems to go over what you sincerely hope is sometimes a clean shirt/blouse.

If you add to this that their hair is never combed and you have even seen them clear up split coffee by wiping a sleeve over the desk, you are now very anxious. Their job is meant to involve making presentations on a quarterly basis to the board of directors about the department's business plans. Your fear is that, although the graduate's calculations and planning are likely to be the best ever, the board will reject the message because of the presenter's appearance.

You have noticed that the rest of the team are shying away from the graduate. They feel slightly in awe of this new intellect but need the graduate to be part of the team, not to work in isolation.

You have asked the graduate to come and see you in 10 minutes' time. He/she probably thinks you want to review their progress and maybe praise the new budget control system. However, you know you have to broach this subject with them before they think their dress is acceptable. After all, you have a reputation to protect as well.

Prepare for the interview.

BRIEF FOR GRADUATE

You are an Economics graduate from an Oxbridge University where you gained a first class honours degree. Many organizations were vying to employ you but you chose this one because of the amount of responsibility they were prepared to give you right from the start. Your family are delighted for you. They used to be quite well-off, but have fallen on hard times and in your lifetime there has never been any money to spare for the niceties of life. Even now, most of what you earn you send back to your family to help out and the rest you save because you want a much more secure financial future.

You were thrilled at the prospect of making presentations to the board of your work on the quarterly business plans, amongst other things. A love of maths, statistics and economics has been your whole life and you feel glad to have found a job that allows you to earn money doing the things you enjoy. At university you spent days and nights on end, locked in your room, searching for the answers to complicated problems. The professors were always terribly impressed with your workings and answers. You never cared much for going out and making friends, especially with the financial restrictions placed upon you by the family.

Much as you have enjoyed the work so far, you are finding the environment very strange. You can't understand the importance everyone attaches to arriving on time and only having coffee at break time – surely you have coffee whenever the brain needs it? As a result you have not found it easy to make friends with your colleagues. You think they are all rather boring and regimented and you are hoping to continue with your work without bothering about them too much.

The boss has asked you to come in for a meeting in 10 minutes. You expect this is part of a review system which was mentioned during recruitment, to monitor your progress. As you have just devised a brilliant adaptation of the budget control system, you are hoping to be praised for saving everyone's time.

Prepare for the interview.

4

Dealing with debt

Aim

To enable participants to practise counselling an employee with a financial problem.

Materials required

- Document 4.1 – Brief for manager
- Document 4.2 – Brief for employee

Background

Debt is an increasing problem. Access to credit is relatively easy and many people have become burdened with large mortgages, loans at high rates of interest and the fear of redundancy.

These are the steps which can be used with problems of debt.

1. Assess the level of the problem – list all income and expenditure. Make sure that obvious costs such as rent/mortgage are included as well as less obvious ones such as dry cleaning, entertainment. The final balance could well be a minus one.

   Many people are too worried to calculate the extent of their commitments.
2. Look at the list and see what items could be reduced – rent for example is normally fixed unless you are willing to move.
3. If there is nothing which can be reduced then more serious measures need to be taken. Prioritize the outgoings – food, household costs, rent, electricity, gas, insurances, pensions, credit cards and accounts.
4. Contact the different creditors and negotiate what you can afford to pay.

Method

Choose one of the four methods described in the Introduction and brief the participants accordingly.

Debriefing

1. Ask the counsellor and then the counsellee for their reactions and feelings.
2. Open the discussion to the whole group asking for feedback on the role play.
3. Use the counselling model to point out any difficulties.
4. Note any points which arise on the flip chart.

Additional guidance

Citizens' Advice Bureau can advise and also supply a number of useful pamphlets.

BRIEF FOR MANAGER

You have just given one of your staff an appraisal. They have done very well and you and the organization are pleased with them. However, for economic reasons there is a freeze on pay increases for six months. You explained this, and although you did not expect the employee to be pleased you were amazed at the anger of the response. You suspect that there is something behind it and have arranged another interview to discuss it.

Prepare for that interview.

BRIEF FOR EMPLOYEE

You have just been told that there are to be no pay increases and you are devastated. You are in debt and the only thing which was keeping you going was the thought that as you had performed particularly well at work you would be given a big increase in salary. You can understand the company's view: business has been poor and a six months' freeze is better than redundancies. But you do not know what to do next.

This is a monthly statement of your standing orders and direct debits. It does not include your living costs – food, travel etc.

Income		**Expenditure**	
Salary	£1050	Mortgage	£650
		Car HP	£150
		Insurances	£50
		Bank loan interest	£75

You have an overdraft of £1000. You have a mortgage of £65,000 on a property which is valued at £90,000.

The problem is that your partner was made redundant six months ago so your income has been halved. The redundancy pay has been spent, as have your savings. At the moment there is no likelihood of your partner finding another job.

You don't know what to do.

The manager asks to see you. Prepare for that interview.

5

Death

Aim

To provide an opportunity for applying counselling skills in bereavement.

Materials required

- Document 5.1 – Brief for manager
- Document 5.2 – Brief for employee

Background

Death can produce feelings of bewilderment, loss, anger, guilt, numbness, futility and often isolation. (This kind of grief can also be felt when there is a different kind of loss such as divorce.)

Society is confused about how to deal with those who have been bereaved. There is a feeling that one should try to 'cheer them up', or help them to 'get over it'. We are programmed to look forward, not back, and after the funeral and the initial messages of sympathy, the person facing a loss can be left completely alone.

Support is important. There need to be time and space to enable the person to talk about their feelings. Initially there can be a feeling of shock and disbelief: 'This is all a bad dream', or 'It's not happening to me.'

The disbelief causes people to continue to talk to their dead partner or imagine they are still there. This is quite normal in a stable person. It is understandable that someone who has been part of your life for a long time should not so easily be removed. Strangely, anger can follow, a feeling some people find disturbing: 'She's left me with the kids and the house and my job.' Guilt is also common: 'I didn't do enough for him; if only I'd got him to see that other specialist', or 'I wish I hadn't rowed with her.' There can be 'unfinished business' – things which were not said or done, closing a rift in a relationship, the once-in-a-lifetime trip which never happened – all these can weigh heavily and depress the bereaved.

Eventually the period of mourning reaches a stage when the death or loss can be accepted. This does not mean that it is forgotten, but that life can continue although in a changed form. The length of time needed for grieving can vary depending on the closeness of the relationship, the circumstances of the death, the person themselves and the support available. It may be helpful to have professional bereavement counselling when the grief is very severe, for example when a long-term partner dies, or when the death has been sudden, especially through violence or by suicide, or when the bereaved is already emotionally fragile or isolated. Professional counselling is usually arranged in the first place through the local GP.

Six months to a year or even two is fairly common for the grieving process to run its course. But without support and a sympathetic ear the grief can remain unresolved indefinitely.

Method

Chose one of the four methods described in the Introduction and brief the participants accordingly.

Debriefing

1. Ask the counsellor and counsellee for their feelings.
2. Next ask the whole group for their reactions and feelings.
3. Use the counselling model to point out any problem areas.
4. Note points which arise on the flip chart.

Additional guidance

This exercise can trigger deep feelings in the counsellee. Make sure they have an opportunity to discuss these if they need to during or after the training session.

BRIEF FOR MANAGER

One of your employees has suffered a bereavement – their partner was killed in a car crash about six weeks ago. They have just come back to work. They seem all right but you need to check how they are feeling. You ask to see them.

Prepare for the interview.

BRIEF FOR EMPLOYEE

You suffered a bereavement about six weeks ago. Your partner was killed in a car crash involving a 'drink driver'. The other driver is being prosecuted by the police. You are faced with being on your own, financial problems, and the trauma of a court case. Tell the manager what is worrying you, how you are managing at home and how this relates to work.

Prepare for the interview.

6

Drugs in the family

Aims

To improve participants' knowledge of drugs and drug issues. To practise counselling someone with a drug-related problem.

Materials required

- Document 6.1 – Background brief (all except room attendant).
- Document 6.2 – Brief for manager, role play I
- Document 6.3 – Brief for manager, role play II
- Document 6.4 – Brief for room attendant, role play I
- Document 6.5 – Brief for housekeeper, role play II

Background

Drugs are not just a problem for TV cops! Substance abuse is found among all types of people, rich and poor, at home and at work.

Drug taking can affect employees in your organization either through their own use or through the use by a partner, relative or close friend.

The main drugs are often classified as follows:

1. 'Soft drugs'
   - *Amphetamines (speed)* White or brown powder, pill or capsule, sniffed or injected. Makes user lively, giggly and over-alert.
   - *Cannabis (pot, dope, hash, grass)* Hard brown resinous material, usually smoked. Produces appearance of being drunk, very talkative.
2. 'Hard drugs'
   - *Cocaine (coke)* Comes from the coca bush, native to the South American Andes. Cocaine in Britain is cocaine hydrochloride, produced by processing coca paste with acids and

- solvents. It takes the form of a white powder. Sniffed, sometimes smoked or injected. Can be smoked through a process known as 'free-basing', when the cocaine is freed from the acid hydrochloride. Users feel alert, energetic, confident, indifferent to pain and fatigue. Does not cause physical dependence but psychological dependence may well develop.
- *Crack* Small bits of free-base cocaine. Smoked in pipes, tinfoil or in cigarettes. Powerful stimulant, increasing heart rate and blood pressure. It produces a 'high' lasting about 12 minutes. Users report after-effects such as depression and anxiety.
- *Heroin (smack, skag)* Heroin is an opiate (a group of drugs derived from the opium poppy). It is a depressant, produced in order to develop a safe (less dependence-producing) drug than morphine. It takes the form of a white powder. Is often mixed (or 'cut') with other substances, so its strength is variable. Can be smoked, sniffed or injected. It is a powerful painkiller and is used to treat cancer and heart attack patients. Heroin makes the user feel contented, drowsy, warm and euphoric. Physical and strong psychological dependency can occur.
- *LSD* Lysergic acid diethylamide, LSD, is the most potent of the commonly available hallucinogens. It is derived from the fungus ergot which grows on rye and other grasses. It is a white powder but available in many forms: capsules, sugar cubes, microdots, tiny stamps (with a flashy design), on blotting paper or as a liquid. It is usually swallowed, but may be sniffed or injected. Reactions can depend to a certain extent on the state of the user. If the company, surroundings and well being of the user are good, then heightened self-awareness, mystical experiences, vivid intensified colours, movement in stationary objects and distortions of space and time can occur. If the user is depressed, then the experiences can include extreme mental disorientation, dizziness, anxiety, more depression and paranoia. A small minority of users become psychologically dependent.
- *Magic mushroom* Fungi found wild. Effects similar to LSD.
- *Opiods (dikes)* Red, white tablets or ampules swallowed or injected. Similar to heroin.

Method

Choose one of the four methods described in the Introduction and brief the participants accordingly.

Note that there are two role plays here:

I. Manager with head housekeeper

II. Manager with room attendant

It is better to assign a different participant for the manager in role plays I and II. Group size, timings and materials needed will therefore have to be adjusted accordingly.

Debriefing

1. For each role play ask the counsellor and the counsellee for their reactions and feelings.
2. Open the discussion to the whole group asking for comments and feelings on how each role play went.
3. Use the counselling model to point out any difficulties.
4. Note any points on the flip chart.
5. Open out the discussion to drugs in general using the company policy if one exists.

(Debriefing can be done either after each role play or after the two.)

Additional guidance

It is important that participants are honest. Although drugs are illegal, a user needs support and help to stop taking them, not punishment.

Your organization may have a policy on drugs. It may offer drug counselling to the employee

- at work
- during paid sick leave
- during unpaid leave
- after dismissal (this may be the only option if the employee refuses help).

BACKGROUND BRIEF

The scene is a 100-room hotel in the centre of a large city. The following conversation takes place between the head housekeeper and the manager about a room attendant (assumed to be male for the purpose of the dialogue):

Housekeeper: He's a good worker, it's just he's been acting oddly recently.

Manager: What do you mean?

Housekeeper: Well, he forgot to turn down the beds in some rooms, didn't clean one bathroom properly, the guest complained, forgot to ask me to order more soaps, so we ran out. Nothing very serious, but he never used to do that.

Manager: Sounds as if he's having some problems. Everything all right at home?

Housekeeper: As far as I know, he hasn't said anything.

Manager: So what do you think is wrong?

Housekeeper: Well it sounds a bit silly. But some of the others have noticed that he's changed. Looks a wreck, clothes dirty, hair never brushed and his skin's come out in blotches and spots.

Manager: Sounds as if he's tired, upset, worried about something.

Housekeeper: It's more than that. Some of the others saw some leaflets about drugs in his locker. I know it sounds a bit dramatic but I think he's on something.

Manager: Are you sure?

Housekeeper: The type – you know, a good worker but likes to party and well, I shouldn't say it, but likes one-night stands.

Manager: I didn't know there was a type.

Housekeeper: You know what I mean. What do you think it is – heroin?

Manager: I don't know. All you've said is he's just not himself.

Housekeeper: I think you'd better have a word.

Manager: It should really be you as the line manager but I'll see him later today and then we can discuss it.

BRIEF FOR MANAGER, ROLE PLAY I

You are the manager of the hotel. You are responsible not only for the running of the hotel, the restaurants and the bars but also for recruiting, disciplining and dismissing staff.

You have asked to see the room attendant. You need to find out:

- how he feels about the standard of his recent work: would he agree that it has fallen?
- what is causing this
- if he is using drugs.

Prepare for that meeting.

BRIEF FOR MANAGER, ROLE PLAY II

You are the manager of the hotel. You are responsible not only for the running of the hotel, the restaurants and the bars but also for recruiting, discipline and dismissing staff.

You now need to talk to the housekeeper. You need to:

- say that you have noticed a drop in the standard of the room attendant's work and that you have spoken to him about it;
- explain what is causing this;
- explain about the drug abuse;
- counsel and advise the housekeeper about the actions needed to help the room attendant;
- suggest that the housekeeper reports back to you regularly.

Prepare for that meeting.

BRIEF FOR ROOM ATTENDANT, ROLE PLAY I

You are a room attendant in a 100-room hotel in the centre of a large city. You usually enjoy the work and take pride in doing the job quickly and well.

You are divorced with two children; Stephen is 15 and Gemma is 10. Stephen has been missing school sometimes; he has been rude and has started fights when he is there, and he has been in some scrapes with some other lads including one where the police gave them a warning. You feel these boys are a bad influence on Stephen.

A few weeks ago you were in his room and you found some cigarettes and in a half-empty packet a bag with white powder in it. You are beside yourself with worry as you think it is cocaine. You are no expert but you have a leaflet from the doctor's surgery which explains some basics. You do not know what to do although you know that you have to talk to Stephen soon and then perhaps, depending on what he says, inform the police.

The manager asks to see you and you know it cannot be good news.

Prepare for the interview.

BRIEF FOR HOUSEKEEPER, ROLE PLAY II

You are the housekeeper of the hotel. You have been asked to see the manager to find out what happened when she/he discussed the problem with the room attendant.

You are quite sure that the attendant is on something. Although a good worker you have never like him. He seemed too keen on having a good time for your liking. Drugs would not surprise you at all; in fact hearing anything else would not ring true. You have decided that the room attendant is a kind of addict and that he will have to go, and you are prepared to say so to the manager. In fact you are very concerned about the possible effect on the younger members of staff, especially if the attendant tries to make money by becoming a 'pusher'.

Prepare for the interview.

7

It's 5 o'clock and I'm off

Aim

To provide an opportunity to meet with an employee who appears to be 'clock-watching'.

Materials required

- Document 7.1 – Brief for manager
- Document 7.2 – Brief for accounts clerk
- Observer's Form
- Personal Action Plan

Background

In some organizations it is the accepted norm either for everyone to leave on time or for everyone to vie for the dubious honour of being the last to leave. In either case, it quickly becomes apparent to everyone when an individual is not pulling their weight, spending more time looking at their watch, taking time off sick and generally not progressing with their work. This role play provides the opportunity to explore ways of bringing the problem into the open and finding out its root causes.

Method

Choose one of the four methods described in the Introduction. Prepare copies of the relevant documents and brief the participants accordingly.

Debriefing

1. Ask the counsellors to comment on what was revealed about their own perceived strengths and weaknesses.

2. Ask the counsellees to say how satisfactory the interview was from their point of view.
3. If using observers, ask them to add anything which has not been covered already, especially if they noticed any significant body language such as the counsellee leaning back with arms folded and head down, or the counsellor not making eye contact, looking nervous etc.
4. Summarize the session by referring back to the counselling model which you are using.
5. Hand out Personal Action Plans for completion.

BRIEF FOR MANAGER

You are the manager of a large and very busy accounts department. You have 3 staff handling the 'payables' and 6 staff handling the 'receivables' as well as 2 trainee accountants and a part-time advisor for VAT and tax issues.

The whole office is kept busy from the moment the phones start ringing at 9.00am until the switchboard closes at 5.30pm. The jobs are all quite pressurized and most of your staff have to deal with a fair proportion of angry callers each day. Lunch is taken on the run and most of your staff stay on after hours to tidy up the books before the start of another day. In a case like this it is vital that everyone takes their share of the work, otherwise the excess falls on the shoulders of the others.

It has come to your notice that one of the team is often seen gazing out of the window, hanging around the coffee machine and being first out of the door at night. As if this wasn't bad enough you have overheard some of the others commenting that they think you are showing favouritism to this person by letting them do less work. On checking the absentee file you discovered that this person takes a high number of odd days off each month.

Obviously something has to be done before the morale of the whole department falls. Also, in view in view of the large amount of time you spend away from your desk at meetings, you need to rely on everyone to pull their weight. Not having time for appraisals means you have to trust that everything is OK until you are told otherwise.

That is why you have asked to see this person first thing in the morning. You haven't said why, knowing you will have to prepare yourself very carefully.

BRIEF FOR ACCOUNTS CLERK

You are one member of the team in a large and busy accounts department. The work seems never-ending. Day after day you are having to deal with complaining customers or suppliers. They always blame you when it is not your fault. So, if you feel you can't face it some days you call in sick.

When you need the boss most, he/she has been called away to a meeting and everyone else is so busy and harassed that you feel totally alone.

This wasn't what you imagined when you responded to the advertisement. After all, the product the company sells is quite exciting and you thought you would be meeting more interesting people and be sent on a course to qualify as an accountant. The boss is so busy you feel completely fed up and haven't had the opportunity to remind him/her about the course. In any case you doubt it will be possible now as there aren't enough people in the department to handle the work effectively at the moment, so how could they do without you for one day a week?

If only the job market weren't so bad at this time of the year with all the school leavers about, you would gladly resign and go elsewhere. The boss has asked to see you in the morning. You don't know why. People haven't been talking to you much lately and you are wondering if you have done something to upset them.

Prepare for the interview.

8

Let's talk about it over dinner

Aims

To provide a forum for opening up the discussion on sexual harassment and reviewing the legal situation if appropriate.

Materials required

- Document 8.1 – Brief for manager
- Document 8.2 – Brief for accuser
- Document 8.3 – Brief for supervisor
- Observer's Form
- Personal Action Plan
- Syndicate rooms

Background

Sexual harassment is a subject which has always existed but has only in recent years been given a name. Interpretation of the term varies widely and as a result accusations can be made which are actually inappropriate. Regardless of the laws concerned, this is an issue which managers are having to learn to deal with no matter how unpleasant or awkward it may be. In this instance the manager has the opportunity to counsel both sides of such a dispute.

The following information applies to the UK only. All employees have rights enshrined in the Employment Protection Act and the Sex Discrimination Act. Sexual harassment is not a criminal offence unless it is actually rape or bodily assault. A proven case of harassment certainly constitutes 'gross misconduct', so it is possible to dismiss the offender on the spot without the usual system of warnings. Of course if the accused does not think this is either true or fair they may bring an action for wrongful dismissal.

On the other hand if a company does not take enough action in the eyes of the accuser, they may resign and then bring an action for constructive dismissal, saying it was impossible to continue working there if no-one took the problem seriously. It is the lack of objective evidence which makes such cases notoriously difficult to prove. Therefore the ability to counsel both parties and arrive at a mutually acceptable view of their understandings, intentions and feelings may save an organization much time, effort and disruption if it can also come to an agreed conclusion.

Method

1. There are two interviews in this role play, so you will need to adapt the method chosen and allow about one and a half hours if not using CCTV. It can be organized with one person playing the manager in both interviews or by rotating the roles. In either case there is the option of having an observer. Explain your choice to the participants and allocate roles.
2. Prepare and distribute copies of documents 8.1, 8.2, 8.3 and the Observer's Form to the relevant participants.
3. Allow 15 minutes for preparation.
4. Ask each group of counsellor, accuser and observer to go to their allocated syndicate rooms and take 20 minutes for the interview plus 5 minutes for a private debriefing.
5. Rotate the role within the syndicate groups and allow a further 10 minutes for preparation.
6. Ask the new groups of counsellor, accused and observer to go back to their syndicate rooms and take 20 minutes for the second interview plus 5 minutes for a private debriefing.

Debriefing

1. Bring all the counselling groups back together and ask the managers to comment both on their views, proposed remedies and how they handled the role play.
2. Ask the counsellees to say how they felt about the interview and its outcome.
3. Ask the observers to add anything else they noticed, both verbal and non-verbal.
4. If appropriate, summarize the laws relating to this case. In circumstances of this kind there is not necessarily one right answer but given the conditions described here, the supervisor is likely to be given a second chance, with a warning noted on file.

BRIEF FOR MANAGER

One of your staff has accused their supervisor of sexual harassment. Before taking the matter any further in the organization, you have decided to interview each one separately to see if the problem can be resolved amicably, without involving the Personnel Department or going to an industrial tribunal.

The company produces micro-chip circuit boards and you staff are 90 per cent female. Therefore it is especially important that you not only treat the problem seriously but that you resolve it to the satisfaction of all. With all the intricate work being done and the ever-present danger of electrical equipment you are conscious that everyone needs peace of mind to concentrate and work safely.

The accuser says that the supervisor offered to take her to supper after work to discuss her personal problems, which were interfering with her work. She says that his behaviour through the evening and at the end, when he suggested the remedy to her problems lay in his bedroom, frightened her into jumping out of his car and taking a taxi home. She wants him dismissed.

The supervisor seems to think he was merely being friendly so you need to examine this and decide if it is a genuine case of harassment by the supervisor or a case of badly mistaken signals from each side. Of course you hope it will all be resolved amicably and that the accuser will agree to see sense.

BRIEF FOR ACCUSER

You are part of a mainly female workforce in a company which produces micro-chip circuit boards. You report to a male supervisor. Unfortunately you have been having a great deal of trouble at home lately. Your son is going through some difficulties as a teenager and your husband is insisting that you stop work to be at home all the time. You have worked all your life, you love it and have no intention of giving it up.

As a result, you have been working very slowly and daydreaming about your conversations with your husband, running over them and working out arguments to use against him.

The supervisor noticed the drop in your output and invited you to supper after work to discuss your problems. You thought he might well be helpful in building your defences against your husband and agreed to go. However, you did lie to your husband about where you were going and with whom, as he would have used it as another reason for you to give up work. You told your supervisor this.

Throughout the meal, he concentrated on your personal relationship and not on the working aspect of the problem. It made you feel uncomfortable but you were pleased to at least be talking with a man who wasn't against you.

When you got into the car outside the restaurant he suggested you go back and spend the night at his place and when you protested that that wasn't why you were there at all, he laughed and said he had understood it was all a ploy to go out with him.

You jumped out of the car as he grabbed at you, and went back into the restaurant to phone for a taxi. Next day you reported the incident to the manager, asking that the supervisor be sacked for gross misconduct. However, you want the manager to be discreet because you don't want your husband to find out. You have been asked to the manager's office for a second interview.

BRIEF FOR SUPERVISOR

You are the supervisor of a mainly female workforce in a company which assembles micro-chip circuit boards. You have always enjoyed working with so many women and secretly hope that they liked the atmosphere which you created. Recently you have noticed that one of them has been daydreaming and not getting on with her work.

You asked if there was a problem and you got the impression it was husband trouble. So, you invited her out to supper so that she could talk about it with you. She said it would have to be right after work so she could find a good excuse to give to her husband. This set you thinking that there was more to this meeting than just worker and supervisor.

During the meal, you asked her about her home life and decided her husband sounded at least 20 years out of date where women are concerned. So, when you got into your car at the end of the evening, you suggested she come home with you for the night. To your surprise, she reacted quite violently and dashed out of the car as you reached across to touch her arm. She yelled something about preferring a taxi.

Next day at work she accused you of sexual harassment and has asked the boss to dismiss you on the spot for gross misconduct. Now it seems to be you who doesn't understand women. The boss has called you in for a meeting to establish your version of the events and presumably decide your fate.

You feel very angry about this, as it was a genuine misunderstanding of the signals on your part and you genuinely have no wish to pay your attentions where they are not wanted.

Prepare to explain yourself.

9

Losing your temper

Aims

To enable participants to counsel someone who is angry about something at work.

Materials required

- Document 9.1 – Background brief (for everyone)
- Document 9.2 – Brief for manager
- Document 9.3 – Brief for Jones
- Document 9.4 – Brief for Ford
- Document 9.5 – Brief for Long

Background

Violent anger is a natural reaction but one which is usually unacceptable at work. Counselling someone who feels like this is in essence no different from counselling in any other circumstances. However, it is important to remain neutral and objective. It is not helpful to take sides nor even to try to act as judge until you have heard the facts and counselled the participants.

Method

Choose one of the four methods described in the Introduction and brief the participants accordingly.

There are four roles:

- Manager
- 'Jones'
- 'Ford'
- 'Long'

The counsellor sees each person individually, so that there are three role plays.

You may want to have the same manager throughout, or to switch the roles amongst the participants.

Whichever method is used group size and suggested timing will need to be altered. (If using Method 4, 'Group of 3' will become 'Group of 5'.)

Briefing

1. Ask the counsellor and counsellees for their feelings.
2. Next ask the group for their reactions and feelings.
3. Using the counselling model point out any problem areas.
4. Note points which arise on the flip chart.

BACKGROUND BRIEF

Dent Office Suppliers are a medium-sized company specializing in stationery for business. They print anything from letter heads and business cards to glossy company brochures and leaflets. They have two sales personnel, Jones and Ford, and an assistant, Long, who deals with admin.

Yesterday there was a massive row in the sales department. Jones completely lost his/her temper, shouting, screaming and tearing up files, and if another member of staff had not been around to calm him/her down would have started on Ford!

BRIEF FOR MANAGER

Interview each member of your sales team separately with the aim of restoring peace.

- Role play 1 – Jones
- Role play 2 – Ford
- Role play 3 – Long

Prepare for the appropriate role plays.

BRIEF FOR JONES

You have been working for Dent for nine moths after a very successful career working for another firm of printers. Although you are only 25 you have a great deal of experience and business sense. You have a good list of clients which you not only maintain but also add to. Everyone is very pleased apart from your colleague Ford. Ford made it clear from the start he/she did not think your experience was relevant and that you were not capable of the job.

Ford and Long have made your life very difficult. They always give their customers priority, and not only that, it often feels as if they are trying to sabotage your efforts. Phone messages are lost or taken incorrectly, orders are delayed or damaged, and company information about discounts or delivery dates often do not reach you on time.

You regret becoming angry with them but you were at the end of your tether. The argument was about your losing a big account because you did not have the support you needed.

The boss has to see you one at a time to resolve the matter.

BRIEF FOR FORD

You have been working for Dent for about eight years, seeing it grow from a small company to its present size. Sales are good and you have a solid customer base. You were not very pleased when Jones was brought in. You did not think there was a need for another person in sales and certainly not someone like Jones. He/she is always in a rush and to your mind never does anything properly. You have systems which have worked fine and you have trained Long in them. But Jones comes along and thinks he/she knows best, wants to change things, 'do it his/her way'. You are twice Jones's age and you have twice as much experience but that does not seem to count for very much.

The argument was quite unnecessary and Jones's reaction was completely out of proportion. As far as you know it seemed to be about one customer who had cancelled an order. Jones seemed to blame you even though everyone knows that these things happen, especially if you rush around like a mad thing.

The boss has asked to see you individually about the argument yesterday. Prepare for the meeting.

BRIEF FOR LONG

You have been working for Dent for about two years. You are quite happy, as your first job from school it is not bad. Ford has been helpful. Ford likes to do things his/her way, but you have learnt much about printing so you are reasonably happy.

Jones is very ambitious and you could see that there was going to be trouble when he/she started working with you and Ford. Jones was ready to listen to Ford's ideas but was not going to follow them unless Jones agreed. You have found your place very difficult. You like Jones but you feel you have some loyalty to Ford. Also if Ford asks you to do something you do not think you can ignore it. So you have sometimes done things which were not very helpful to Jones because you have been told to by Ford.

You are very glad to have the opportunity to meet with the boss as you can talk about your worries. Prepare.

10

Mistakes cost money

Aims

To provide an opportunity to deal with the sensitive issue of waste.

Materials required

- Document 10.1 – Brief for manager
- Document 10.2 – Brief for team members
- Observer's Form
- Personal Action Plan

Background

All organizations have accounting systems such as purchase orders and sales invoices. However, what is more difficult to trace is the part of those monies which disappear due to ineffective usage of materials, processes and accidental or thoughtless wastage. This role play enables managers to practise addressing this issue and thereby avoid making any accusations when faced with the reality. It addresses the problem with the team as a whole rather than singling out any specific individuals.

Method

1. This is a 'team meeting' role play where the manager has to use counselling skills with a group of people. Decide who is to take the role of manager and who will be the observer. The remainder can then take the roles of the team workers.
2. Prepare copies of the relevant documents and distribute them accordingly. Allow 10 minutes for study and preparation.
3. Ask the manager to begin and allocate 20 minutes for this 'team counselling' session.

Debriefing

1. Ask the manager how they felt about the meeting. What did it achieve in their view?
2. Ask the team members to say how they felt.
3. Ask the observer to add anything else they noticed.
4. Summarize by comparing the manager's behaviour to the model of counselling which you are using and also to any company procedures regarding budgetary control.
5. Hand out Personal Action Plans for completion.

BRIEF FOR MANAGER

You manage a group of three or four people in an organization where there are very tight budgets for direct and indirect production costs as well as all the general office supplies.

In the last six months, you have found that, among other things, the supplies cupboard needs replenishing much more often than was usual. You suspect that the staff have become complacent since your last pep-talk and therefore wasteful with paperclips and telephone time etc. They don't seem to realize that every penny has to be accounted for to the financial controller.

Rather than become a detective and try to identify those responsible, you have decided to open up the problem with the team and see how they feel. Do they realize there is a problem and how serious it is? What solutions might they propose?

You will be holding this meeting in the coffee room in 10 minutes' time, so prepare yourself.

BRIEF FOR TEAM MEMBERS

You are one of a team of three or four people reporting to the manager who has asked you all to attend a meeting in the coffee room. You don't know what it is about, but the manager looked serious and muttered something about cost controls.

You don't exactly have a guilty conscience but you are wondering if the manager has noticed that (choose one):

1. You have been throwing away a great many photocopies lately – it's not your fault the machine keeps producing faulty copies.
2. You left behind a box of felt tipped pens you took to a conference.
3. You have been spending a long time talking to some of the customers on the phone.
4. You threw away all your old files and made up a new set so as to keep control of the paperwork.
5. You are printing out all your electronic messages so you can take action and file them later.
6. You keep copies of all your assistant's outgoing mail on your files too.

So, prepare for this meeting about cost control, whose responsibility it is and how you may contribute to it.

11

Moonlighting

Aims

To provide an opportunity to practise counselling someone who is not performing well at work without knowing the reason why.

Materials required

- Document 11.1 – Brief for manager
- Document 11.2 – Brief for employee
- Observer's Form
- Personal Action Plan

Background

When someone is not performing well at work there are many possible causes – lack of training, personal worries, lack of motivation, insufficient tools, ill-health, perfectionism etc. In this case, the counsellee is actually tired out from doing a second job out of usual working hours. The manager has to find out what the problem is, using their counselling skills, and help the counsellee find a solution.

Note: In some organizations the contract of employment specifically prohibits this. Check the facts on this and on overtime payments before starting this role play so that you can bring the relevant regulations to everyone's attention in the debriefing.

Method

Choose one of the four methods described in the Introduction. Prepare copies of the relevant documents and brief the participants accordingly.

Debriefing

1. Ask the manager what they identified the problem as. Then ask them to comment on their own performance as a counsellor.
2. Ask the counsellee how they were treated and to add any comments about the manager's counselling skills.
3. If observers were used, ask for their views, not forgetting body language.
4. Relate what has happened back to your model of counselling skills and highlight the reasons for success or failure in this instance.
5. If appropriate, inform participants of the organization's policy on employees having a second job and also anything relevant to overtime payments in case one of the 'managers' has offered this as a solution.
6. Hand out Personal Action Plans for completion.

BRIEF FOR MANAGER

You are the manager of a team of people who, until now, have been performing well. However, you have started to notice one particular individual who, whenever you pass by, is either gazing out of the window, looking exhausted or has gone for another coffee.

When you requested the return of some delegated work, they looked surprised and admitted that they hadn't actually started it. This made you feel angry at first, but then you thought 'Oh well, this is Monday, maybe they had a really exciting weekend'. So you decided not to say anything right away. But now, it has been going on for at least two weeks and you are concerned that something is seriously wrong.

You have asked this person to come into your office for a chat in 10 minutes. Prepare what you are going to say and do to identify the problem and solve it.

BRIEF FOR EMPLOYEE

You are a member of a working team who all depend upon each other to keep the work under control. You are aware that you have been letting them down lately because you have not been at your best. Two weeks ago, you took on a bar job at night in order to bring in some extra cash to the household. Since having an elderly relative move in with you, the budget has become very strained. You imagined that bar work would be as easy as sitting on the other side drinking, but it turns out to be physically very tiring indeed. No break during three and a half hours and always on your feet. Added to that you are breathing in all that unaccustomed smoke and you feel dreadful each morning.

You have told a couple of your colleagues who have been very understanding and have been trying to cover up for you where possible. You appreciate this, but know it is not their problem.

Now, the boss is asking to see you. You are expecting a warning at the very least. You are starting to feel desperate, backed into a corner and if the boss is even slightly accusatory you are likely to snap and shout or become upset.

Prepare for the interview.

12

New owners

Aim

To provide a forum for counselling an employee experiencing organizational change.

Materials required

- Document 12.1 – Brief for manager
- Document 12.2 – Brief for employee

Background

The management of change becomes necessary when a company faces a new operating procedure, new competition, a redefinition of business aims or when rationalization or expansion takes place, including takeover by another organization. Takeovers can be extremely unsettling for employees, even if they see it is a good step for the organization. There is the fear of redundancy, new working practices, an alien culture, different mix of people in new teams and the worst fear of all – the unknown.

Counselling is very important to maintain morale and motivation, and prevent the good employees from resigning.

Method

Choose one of the four methods described in the Introduction and brief the participants accordingly.

Debriefing

1. Ask the counsellor and counsellee for their feelings.
2. Next ask the whole group for their reactions and feelings.
3. Use the counselling model to point to problem areas.
4. Note points which arise on the flip chart.

BRIEF FOR MANAGER

Your organization is about to be taken over by a rival company based overseas. In the long term this should be good for you and your staff in terms of:

- increased market share
- reduced overheads and so higher profits
- expansion of R&D
- opportunities to travel and work abroad.

At the moment senior management have made these commitments:

1. No redundancies will occur for the next 12 months although jobs may be lost through natural wastage.
2. Within two years sites will be amalgamated. All work will be centralized in an existing or new building or plant not more than ten miles from current sites.
3. The same teams will carry on working together for the next six months and after that changes will be kept to the minimum.
4. There will be opportunities for travel and work overseas although no-one will be forced to take up this offer.

Prepare for an interview with one of your staff.

BRIEF FOR EMPLOYEE

Your organization is about to be taken over by a rival company based overseas.

Choose three points from the list below to discuss with the manager. Try to choose ones which might worry you in real life.

1. Redundancy – you have been with the company for 13 years. Under the existing agreement you would be given a large cash sum, enough for you to realize your dream of opening a restaurant.
2. You are close to retirement and you are terrified that if you are made redundant you will spend three years in misery before you can draw your pension.
3. You have been with the organization for 18 months and under the existing rules you would only receive minimal redundancy payments. You do not want to wait for this but would rather have a secure future in another company. You want to know what your chances are of being kept on so that you can plan your future.
4. You do not want to move to another country, although you are happy to move within your own country.
5. You have strong local commitments – family, friends, property etc – and do not want to move to another part of the country.
6. You hate where your company is based and would like to move, especially to another country.
7. You are working on a very interesting project with a good team. If this is going to be wrecked by the takeover you would rather leave and find another job.
8. The team you are working with lacks expertise. You are sure that the rival company will have more experience and you think this will give it a real boost.
9. You are worried about your career. You had a good future mapped out but with double the number of staff you may not get on so fast.
10. You are head of a department. When the takeover happens you will probably be demoted. You wonder about leaving to study for an MBA rather waiting for the inevitable to happen.

Your manager wants to talk to you about what the takeover will mean for you. Use this opportunity to talk about your worries.

Tg

13

On the scrap heap

Aim

To enable managers to practise counselling skills with an employee who has been made redundant.

Materials required

- Document 13.1 – Brief for manager
- Document 13.2 – Brief for employee
- Observer's Form
- Personal Action Plan

Background

Making someone redundant is one of the most difficult tasks facing managers today. At one time it was a rare occurrence, but that is no longer the case. When a manager and team have worked together for a long time, it is a difficult task, choosing who has to go. Response to the news needs very careful handling for the emotional well-being of both parties. This role play gives managers a chance to practise and therefore be well prepared for the reality.

In the UK redundancy is covered by the Employment Protection (Consolidation) Act 1978. It is defined as when:

- the firm closes
- the business is taken over
- the firm moves
- the employee's work is reduced
- the employee is laid off or put on short time.

There are rules covering qualification for protection by redundancy law such as length of service and there is a statutory minimum scale of payments to be made. Industrial tribunals expect employers to follow five principles when making redundancies and will take them into consideration if an employee brings an action for unfair dismissal:

1. Give as much warning as possible.
2. Consult with any union on the selection criteria.
3. Use objective criteria such as attendance record and length of service, not personal opinions about personality.
4. Follow the criteria closely.
5. Check no alternative jobs are available.

Method

Choose one of the four methods described in the Introduction. Prepare copies of the relevant documents and brief the participants accordingly.

Debriefing

1. Ask the managers to comment on their own performance.
2. Ask the employees to comment on their feelings during this session and how they were dealt with.
3. If using observers, ask for any additional comments they may have, adding your own in relation to any model of counselling you have been using.
4. Ensure that all praise is accepted by the managers and that all criticisms are noted in a positive way for future development.
5. Hand out Personal Action Plans for completion.

BRIEF FOR MANAGER

You have been instructed to make one of two people working for you redundant and it has been very difficult to decide between them. You don't want to lose either of them as they both contribute to the company in different ways.

The person you are keeping is 28 and married, but with no family as yet. He/she is very dedicated and professional about their career and have been with the company about five years. He/she is following a business studies course with the Open University and know where they are going in the organization. They are very comfortable with teamwork and the political demands of a corporate environment.

The person you have made redundant is a single person 45 years old. This is a creative individual who always brings a fresh way of looking at issues but does not play the 'corporate game'. During the last five years their work has always been of a very high standard but you are aware that they are becoming bored with the job. Unfortunately, there is nothing else available within the company which would make use of their undoubted ability to accept new challenges and tackle them with enthusiasm.

Your redundant member of staff has asked for this meeting with you. It is their last day at the office since being given the news a month ago. You are not aware of their having had any time off for interviews, but know that the redundancy package will provide about six months' living expenses.

BRIEF FOR EMPLOYEE

You are a single person 45 years old. Your career to date has been full of travel and new experiences. You joined this company five years ago and although you enjoyed the initial challenge, you really want something new now. Everything you have done has been a great success. In fact you were always top of the class and have never failed at anything YOU wanted to do.

You realize that someone had to be made redundant in your department and you assumed it would be your younger colleague. When your boss gave you the news you were very surprised and for the last three or four weeks you have been letting it sink in whilst starting to question the basis for the decision. Why you? Is it because you are over 40? Has your work not been as appreciated as much as it seemed at appraisal time? Does the boss feel more threatened by you than by your younger colleague? Don't they like your creative and objective approach to things? Do they prefer the more company line taken by your colleague? All of this has been on your mind and you have been interrupting your colleagues to talk it over. Someone has suggested you have a meeting with your boss to find out the reason, for your own peace of mind.

You are feeling a mixture of hurt, anger and worry. After all, what chance does anyone have of getting a new job these days when they are over 40?

14

Out to grass

Aim

To provide a forum for discussion of the problems people face when presented with the opportunity of taking early retirement.

Materials required

- Document 14.1 – Brief for manager
- Document 14.2 – Brief for employee
- Observer's Form
- Personal Action Plan

Background

The chance to retire early is something many people crave. They see it as a chance to do more with their time, for example, improve their golf handicap, take flying lessons, spend time in the garden or learn a new language. However, not everyone sees it that way, especially if the person concerned has made their work their life. When such a person is given early retirement, it can be such a blow that careful counselling is needed to ensure that they don't become depressed or de-motivate their colleagues before they go. This role play provides the opportunity for the various issues and avenues of help to be identified and discussed.

Before beginning such an interview in reality the manager might like to investigate the sources of help in the community which will become available to the employee when they are on their own. For example, the Citizens' Advice Bureau, the local Adult Education College, the Social Security office and lists of clubs from the library, may be helpful.

Method

Chose one of the four methods described in the Introduction. Prepare copies of the relevant documents and brief the participants accordingly.

Debriefing

1. Ask the managers how they felt. What help were they able to offer and what is company policy on these matters?
2. Ask the counsellees how they felt about the interview. Did it help, were they offered suitable guidance?
3. Ask the observers (if used) to comment on anything additional they have seen or heard in the interviews.
4. Summarize the session in two ways. First, refer back to the model of counselling skills you have discussed with the participants. Second, make sure everyone is aware of company policy on early retirement: what actual help can be offered and where people can be directed for further guidance or counselling if necessary.
5. Hand out Personal Action Plans for completion.

BRIEF FOR MANAGER

In order to reduce the headcount in your department you have chosen the oldest member of your staff for early retirement. In fact you wish it could have been yourself as you have many hobbies and interests you would like to pursue. Therefore you expected this person to be very grateful and you were extremely surprised when they took it so badly.

This person is two years away from their natural retirement age. The company is offering a full pension for these two years plus the equivalent of a redundancy package as a lump sum to cushion the blow.

You had planned a leaving party for them but suddenly they have said they don't want it as the company obviously doesn't want them. As a result you have asked if they would like to join you for lunch at a quiet but exclusive local restaurant to talk it over. You will need to be prepared for a potentially difficult and even tearful time.

-BRIEF FOR EMPLOYEE

You are two years away from your natural retirement age and never imagined things would be any different. Therefore it came as a great shock when your boss called you in to the office and told you that, in view of the need for cutbacks, you had been chosen for early retirement. It is not actually a redundancy as your job will still be done, just divided up between two of the younger staff.

You didn't say anything at the time because of the shock but you have now started to feel bitter and disappointed. You have put your whole life into this company and you had always looked forward to leaving with your long service certificate and a jolly party. Now it seems you will narrowly miss that certificate and a merely ordinary party is being planned which you see as a way of dispensing with you.

When you mentioned your feelings to the boss you were invited to go to lunch at an admittedly rather expensive local restaurant specifically to talk over the situation away from the office environment. You are planning to make it quite clear that you feel hurt and rejected. You feel you are being denied the right to complete your natural length of service to the company after you have given the job your total dedication.

The company has offered you a full pension immediately and a redundancy-type package as a lump sum. The trouble is, you have no idea how you might spend either the money or the time.

Prepare for the interview.

15

Passed over

Aim

To enable participants to practise counselling for career planning.

Materials required

- Document 15.1 – Brief for senior manager
- Document 15.2 – Brief for junior manager

Background

Managers may sometimes be forced to make decisions which mean that junior staff are promoted over more senior staff. This can cause resentment and demotivation. The manager will need to counsel the staff member who has been passed over.

Method

Choose one of the four methods described in the Introduction and brief the participants accordingly.

Debriefing

1. Ask the senior manager-counsellor and then the junior manager-counsellee for their reactions and feelings.
2. Open the discussion to the whole group asking them for their own feelings and other suggestions for how the role play could have been dealt with.
3. Use the counselling model to explore ways of improving.
4. Note points which arise on the flip chart.
5. Discuss the company's policy if relevant.

BRIEF FOR SENIOR MANAGER

You are a senior manager in a tax planning and consultancy practice, Fleecem, Fleecem and Avoidem. You are in charge of tax planning for individuals who are usually home-based but are temporarily working abroad. It is a flourishing area. Despite the slump in business from the Middle East caused by the Gulf War, you have made inroads in your field in the Far East – China, Taiwan and Thailand. Developments in the former Soviet Union countries also show potential for your planning and consultancy services.

You have three junior managers in your team:

- A is 50 years old and joined the firm in 1980. A is a qualified accountant but did additional training to become a tax adviser. A had his/her own practice but unfortunately went bankrupt through clients' bad debts and as a result lost their home and savings. This was when they joined the firm. Previous to that A had worked for a number of years in Egypt and Saudi Arabia so speaks Arabic and has a good grasp of the Arab culture. A is responsible for the Middle East business in the department. A is married with three children – 14, 16, 18. A's partner was a teacher, but now stays at home teaching private students. Their youngest child Richard has Down's Syndrome and needs constant supervision; when A's partner is not there they have to use expensive agency nurses.
- B is 35 years old and recently joined the firm from Hong Kong as a tax lawyer. B was born in mainland China but trained and qualified in Hong Kong. B speaks Cantonese, Mandarin and some Japanese and Thai. B's speciality is the Far East practice. B is divorced but lives with an oil trader.
- C is 36 years old and recently joined from a rival firm. C is a qualified accountant and tax lawyer. C has trained both in the UK and the USA. In addition C has taught at a university in Boston before going back into practice. C's parents are Polish and C speaks Polish and Russian. C has a flair for languages and also speaks German, French and Spanish. C is responsible for Europe. C is single.

The situation

You have been allowed an increase in headcount to take an assistant manager into the team. One of your junior managers will be promoted to a higher grade and given the new member of staff to be responsible for.

You have discussed the changes with the partner in charge and have come to the conclusion that C should be promoted and given the new member of staff to train up and work in their team.

European business is growing fast, with the changes in the old Soviet Union, and C is ideal to take up that challenge. He/she has the experience and the skills not only to increase the business but also to train a new member of staff.

A is an Arab specialist and at the moment that business merely ticks over; there is no need to expand that area. If he/she were to be given new responsibilities there would be a significant learning curve of new languages to be dealt with. A also has not had the appropriate experience to act as a trainer. The decision has not been made because of a lack of ability.

B could probably develop more business but, in terms of priority, Europe and Russia represent a more pressing market. You envisage expanding B's role in 6 to 12 months' time. Your choice is no reflection on their ability.

You have told the three managers of your decision and have begun recruiting a new member of staff. You thought that everyone was happy until you overheard the following conversation in the canteen between A and Julie, A's long-time secretary.

A: It's so unfair.
Julie: I know. I couldn't believe it when the boss announced it.
A: C's not out of nappies yet. I mean, what do people like that know about the real world? They spent most of their time in some academic ivory tower.
Julie: Cocky, that's for sure. And they wouldn't know a joke if they fell over one.
A: I know why the boss turned me down, too.
Julie: Yeah.
A: It's because I had to take that time off when we couldn't find a nurse to look after Richard.
Julie: Do you think that was what it was?
A: Sure of it.
Julie: That's awful, after all you've gone through for that boy too. How is he, anyway?
A: Oh he's doing really well at this new day centre. He loves it.
Julie: That's good.
A: It's not fair. I deserve the promotion and I need the money much more than old clever clogs does.
Julie: Yeah. Tight-fisted or what? Never seems to spend any of it.
A: Never gets a chance. Always at work, creeping to the partners.
Julie: You should have it out with the boss. Don't let them walk all over you!

A: You're right. I'll go in there and have it out. At the very least I deserve a rise after all I've done for the firm.

You are therefore not surprised when A storms into your office and demands a rise.

Prepare to deal with this.

BRIEF FOR JUNIOR MANAGER

A – You joined Fleecem, Fleecem and Avoidem, a tax planning and consultancy practice, in 1980. Your work involves planning for individuals who are usually home-based but are temporarily working abroad. It is a flourishing area, despite the slump in business from the Middle East caused by the Gulf War. Your department has made inroads in your speciality work in the Far East – China, Taiwan and Thailand. Developments in the former Soviet Union also show potential for the department's planning and consultancy services.

You are 50 years old, a qualified accountant who did additional training to become a tax adviser when you joined the firm. You had your own practice but unfortunately you went bankrupt through clients' bad debts and as a result lost your home and savings. This was why you joined the firm. Previous to that you worked for a number of years in Egypt and Saudi Arabia so speak Arabic and have a good grasp of the Arab culture. You are responsible for the Middle East business in the department.

You are married with three children – 14, 16, 18. Your partner was a teacher, but now stays at home teaching private students.

Your youngest child, Richard, has Down's Syndrome and needs constant supervision. When your partner is not there you have to use expensive agency nurses.

Other members of your department are the senior manager, in charge of the three junior managers, of whom you are the oldest although the same in grade; yourself and the other junior managers, B and C.

B is 35 years old and recently joined the firm from Hong Kong where they were a tax lawyer. B was born in mainland China but trained and qualified in Hong Kong. B speaks Cantonese, Mandarin and some Japanese and Thai. B's speciality is the Far East practice. B is divorced but lives with an oil trader.

C is 36 years old and recently joined from a rival firm. C is a qualified accountant and tax lawyer. C has trained both in the UK and the USA. In addition C has taught at a university in Boston before going back into practice. C's parents are Polish and speaks Polish and Russian. C has a flair for languages and also speaks German, French and Spanish. C is responsible for Europe. C is single.

Your manager has been allowed an increase in headcount to take an assistant manager into the team. One of the junior managers, which includes you, will be promoted to the next higher grade and given the new member of staff to be responsible for.

The senior manager has discussed the changes with the partner in charge and they have come to the conclusion that your colleague C should be promoted and given the new member of staff to train up and work in their team.

Soon afterwards you have this conversation with Julie, your long-time secretary.

A: It's so unfair.
Julie: I know. I couldn't believe it when the boss announced it.
A: C's not out of nappies yet. I mean, what do people like that know about the real world? They spent most of their time in some academic ivory tower.
Julie: Cocky, that's for sure. And they wouldn't know a joke if they fell over one.
A: I know why the boss turned me down, too.
Julie: Yeah.
A: It's because I had to take that time off when we couldn't get a nurse to look after Richard.
Julie: Do you think that was what it was?
A: Sure of it.
Julie: That's awful, after all you've gone through for that boy too. How is he, anyway?
A: Oh he's doing really well at this new day centre. He loves it.
Julie: That's good.
A: It's not fair. I deserve the promotion and I need the money much more than old clever clogs does.
Julie: Yeah. Tight-fisted or what? Never seems to spend any of it.
A: Never gets a chance. Always at work, creeping to the partners.
Julie: You should have it out with the boss. Don't let them walk all over you!
A: You're right. I'll go in there and have it out. At the very least I deserve a rise after all I've done for the firm.

You decide to act at once. Prepare yourself for the meeting with your boss.

16

Petty theft

Aim

To enable participants to practise counselling where petty theft is involved.

Materials required

- Document 16.1 – Brief for head of department
- Document 16.2 – Brief for Pat Strachan

Background

Most organizations have a disciplinary code which covers an employee caught committing a crime. However, most of these codes need some interpretation. It is necessary to decide how serious the breach is, what the past history is and the circumstances in which the breach occurs.

Method

Choose one of the four methods described in the Introduction and brief the participants accordingly.

Debriefing

1. Ask the counsellor and counsellee for their feelings.
2. Open up to the whole group for their reactions and feelings.
3. Use the counselling model to explain any problems which may have been noted.
4. Write any points on the flip chart.
5. A follow-up activity could be a discussion on the 'grey areas' of petty theft such as making personal calls during work time, or 'borrowing' stationery to use at home.

Additional guidance

Your organization may have a policy on theft which you may want to introduce.

BRIEF FOR HEAD OF DEPARTMENT

You are the head of the systems support department. Your job is to maintain hardware and to install small systems within your organization. You have ten engineers and two office staff.

Pat Strachan is one of your senior engineers. Pat is a good worker, punctual and polite, and you have trusted Pat with some of the more important and difficult projects.

It has therefore come as a shock when you happen to drive past your offices one Sunday and see Pat stealing. You are replacing some electronic typewriters with personal computers which can be used for word processing as well as spreadsheets and database storage. You are amazed to see Pat loading six of these old typewriters into a car.

You have a policy that anything which is not required any longer by the organization has to be sold. First of all it is advertised internally so that any member of staff has the chance to buy it. If no member of staff is interested, it is sold to a company specializing in second-hand computer equipment. These typewriters have not been advertised. Pat knows this and so is obviously breaking company policy and the action amounts to theft.

You arrange to see Pat.

BRIEF FOR PAT STRACHAN

You work for the Systems Support Department of your company as an engineer. You have to maintain hardware and have recently been involved in installing small systems.

You are one of the senior engineers, a good worker. The Head of Department has trusted you with some of the more important and difficult projects.

Your latest job was to replace some electronic typewriters with personal computers which can be used for word processing as well as spreadsheets and database storage.

You did not think anyone would want the six old typewriters – most people want computers. But you do some charity work with a school for physically handicapped and you know they would be able to make use of the machines.

The company has a policy that anything which is not required any longer by the organization has to be sold. First of all it is advertised internally so that any member of staff has the chance to buy it. If no-one is interested, it is sold to a company specializing in second-hand computer equipment. These typewriters have not been advertised but you are sure that no-one wants them. They are worth virtually nothing and you know that the organization would be happy to give them away for a good cause. Some examinations are due, so the school is in desperate need of them. Rather than become involved with bureaucratic procedures, one evening you loaded the typewriters into your car to deliver to the school the next day.

Somehow the managing director has heard something and has asked to see you to explain. Prepare what you are going to say.

17

Presenting problem

Aim

To provide an opportunity to counsel a colleague on their apparent difficulties with presentation skills.

Materials required

- Document 17.1 – Brief for counsellor
- Document 17.2 – Brief for counsellee
- Observer's Form
- Personal Action Plan

Background

For some people, making a presentation is such a stressful experience that they tend to block out the memory of how they performed, and are just grateful that they lived though it. Unfortunately, those to whom it was made may have rather more vivid memories and a lack of skills in this area could adversely affect someone's career. It is during a presentation that many people are most exposed to senior management. If they don't make a good impression then, their chances of progress can be damaged. This role play is aimed at offering discreet help to a colleague to sort out his or her problems.

Method

Choose one of the four methods described in the Introduction. Prepare copies of the relevant documents and brief the participants accordingly.

Debriefing

1. Ask the counsellor for impressions from their point of view. Did they offend their colleague or was the outcome positive?
2. Ask the counsellee how they felt. Did it help or did they feel like the accused in a hopeless case?
3. Ask the observers for any additional comments.
4. Relate what has happened to the model of counselling which you are using.
5. Hand out the Personal Action Plan for completion.

BRIEF FOR COUNSELLOR

Yesterday you attended the third presentation given by a colleague and in your opinion it was no better than the first. So much for practice making perfect! A few words with your colleague after the presentation made you realize just what a trial it is for him/her. He/she was still shaking, looked quite flushed, had no idea of the time and kept saying 'Thank goodness that's over for another week'.

Thinking back over the presentation itself, you have started to identify some specific problems, for example:

- having a full script on loose sheets of A4 paper which got mixed up;
- leaving the overhead projector beam on even when not in use, and walking through it;
- not distributing an agenda which meant a lot of people started looking at their watches after half an hour;
- staring at the ceiling, the floor and out of the window, but never looking at the audience;
- pacing up and down, hands in pockets.

As a good friend and colleague you feel it is your duty to do something to help so you have suggested a meeting. You are not sure if your intervention will be well received. It could look rather like one-upmanship.

Prepare your counselling session.

BRIEF FOR COUNSELLEE

You have recently been required to make a weekly presentation to all staff about the organization's progress. You have never had training in this field, but didn't like to ask for any in case it made you look foolish or inadequate. Anyway, anyone with an ounce of commonsense can surely cope with a presentation, can't they?

You have tried to avoid errors by writing out a full script like a speech, but last week you dropped the pages and everything became muddled up. It was intensely embarrassing, and you found it very hard to get back on track.

As for that internal overhead projector, even you are confused when you look at those sheets of figures the boss's secretary gives you as acetates to use. Your theory is to rattle through it as quickly as possible because everyone must know that this is just another of those 'good ideas' someone had about communications which is bound to die the death before long. Still, if only you felt more confident ...

A colleague has suggested having a chat with you about the presentations. You are not entirely sure of what their motives are but feel you may as well go along and see.

Prepare for the interview.

18

Sales performance

Aim

To provide an opportunity for practising a post-sales call interview with a salesperson.

Materials required

- Document 18.1 – Brief for sales manager
- Document 18.2 – Brief for salesperson
- Observer's Form
- Personal Action Plan

Background

Top-performing salespeople are sometimes rewarded with a promotion which takes them out of the realm of their personal excellence – selling – and into the unfamiliar territory of managing people. Helping salespeople refine their skills and perform at top level is the main responsibility of any sales manager. So, an opportunity to practise these skills in a non-threatening environment can be invaluable for both new and experienced sales managers.

Method

Choose one of the four methods described in the Introduction. Prepare copies of the relevant documents and brief the participants accordingly.

Debriefing

1. Ask the sales manager how they think the interview went. Did they allow the salesperson to talk, did they gain agreement on future

development and is there anything they would like to have done differently.

2. Ask the salespeople to comment on the interview. Were they allowed to analyse their own performance and are they satisfied with the outcome?
3. Ask the observers to comment on anything else including relevant body language.
4. Refer back to any model for 'kerbside' or post-call interviewing which has been discussed and identify which elements of it were covered in these role plays.
5. Hand out copies of the Personal Action Plan for completion.

BRIEF FOR SALES MANAGER

You are a sales manager with a team of six salespeople reporting in to you. You are expected to spend at least two days a month with each one, communicating about new products, policies and procedures, making joint visits to customers and analysing their performance during a kerbside interview in the car or back at their base, which may identify a need for additional training.

You have come out of a meeting with a big customer whose follow-up orders have been dropping sharply over the last three months. After greeting the customer you sat quietly, listening and observing what was going on during the interview:

- a great deal of time was spent on small talk before any discussion of business;
- when the customer made objections, the salesperson didn't have the answers ready, which was surprising, as it was about one of those new hi-tech models;
- to close the sale, the salesperson said 'So, do you need any more this month, then?' and the answer had been a polite 'No' before you were both ushered out.

Now you have to raise these observations with the salesperson to see if they perceive any problems and how to rectify them. Prepare for the interview.

BRIEF FOR SALESPERSON

You have made a sales call to one of the biggest customers on your patch, though you realize that their orders have been dropping off lately. Your boss, the sales manager, has been with you today and you are both on your way back to the car. He is bound to ask you why you didn't get an order.

As far as you are concerned, you have a very good personal relationship with this customer. You know all about the family and their holiday plans and you make sure you mention them every time. In addition, the fact that his customer is a gardener makes the weather another good ice-breaker.

These new lines they have been buying are very complicated technically and you have never found the time to study them carefully so you can't always answer detailed questions.

With a good customer like this there is no longer any need to close the sale. After all, they know the product well enough by now and will make their own decision, won't they?

You are becoming rather fed up with this sales manager, who used to be one of the team but now seems to try to be superior all the time. So if any kind of training course is mentioned you are likely to be defensive about it and maybe take your chance to say what you have been thinking about these joint calls.

19

Sharing an office

Aim

To give managers the opportunity to use their counselling skills in a group where mediation is required between two parties.

Materials required

- Document 19.1 – Brief for manager
- Document 19.2 – Brief for advertising executive
- Document 19.3 – Brief for project co-ordinator
- Observer's Form
- Personal Action Plan

Background

When office sharing is arranged, people are usually placed together because of a connection in their job function and not because of any particular capacity they may have for working well in close proximity to each other. Outside of our work environment, we all choose who to be close to for a wide variety of reasons; however, in the office we are not necessarily in control of that process. Therefore differences do arise which can result in lost productivity due to simmering resentment or outright aggression. A manager could become aware of the problem in a number of ways. For example:

1. It becomes apparent that work is not reaching the required standards.
2. An argument is observed by all in the office.
3. One of the office sharers makes a formal complaint.

In the first two cases it is the manager who initiates the counselling meeting. In the third case it is the main sufferer who asks for help. This role play is written as if the manager is requesting the meeting but you can adapt your instructions to the participants if you wish them to enact the alternative beginning.

Method

This role play has the manager counselling and mediating between two members of staff together, in the same meeting. Choose one of the four methods in the Introduction. Adapt the timings, prepare copies of the relevant documents and brief the participants accordingly.

Debriefing

1. Ask the managers to comment on their own performance – what they did well and where they found the interview difficult.
2. Ask all the counsellees how they felt about the meeting. Were their differences resolved? Were they bullied? Were they encouraged to come up with a mutually agreed solution?
3. Ask the observers to add any comments which have not already been covered in relation to the 'model' of counselling skills which is being used for comparison.
4. Be encouraging and supportive to the counsellors at all times and remind participants that when dealing with people there are not necessarily going to be absolutely right and wrong answers to a question. With practice, though, they can help people to reach an acceptable compromise.
5. Hand out copies of the Personal Action Plan for completion.

BRIEF FOR MANAGER

You are the sales and marketing manager at Fast Foods International Ltd. The company started as a family business, making sandwiches and buffet lunches for the local factory sites. By word of mouth the business expanded and equipment was installed to produce 'cook-chill' meals for sale in the local supermarkets. You were hired to expand this even further and with your own contacts and sales expertise have won an important contract from one of the national hypermarket chains. Therefore you have a personal interest in ensuring the success of this new venture.

You are responsible for market research, new product development, advertising and sales, plus liaison with purchasing and production. The two sales reps are out on the road most of the time. They share a desk and phone in the main office as they are usually in on different days. They also have a filing cabinet each for their records. Your secretary takes messages for them and passes them on when they phone in each day.

You have two assistants. One is the projects co-ordinator and the other is the advertising executive. They share an office and a secretary who you have noticed has not been looking her usual cheerful self lately.

At a weekly project progress meeting you are horrified to discover that TV advertising has been booked to announce the launch of the new 'No-Fat Hamburger' but that supplies of the new, secret ingredient will not be available until a fortnight later than planned. The sales reps are distressed because they have prepared all their major retailers to make a prominent display at the meat counters, knowing they would be backed up by the advertising campaign. This could be a disaster because the impact of the new product would be completely lost if it were not available when the customers come in looking for it.

The project co-ordinator suddenly shouts that it is the secretary's fault for not having passed the message on sooner. The advertising executive angrily shouts back that it is hardly fair to blame the poor confused secretary when it is clearly the project co-ordinator's workstyle which is at fault – a messy desk, talking loudly on the phone which is very disturbing, and piles of paperwork all over the office. So, it is not at all surprising that something has finally gone wrong.

The project co-ordinator is about to start yelling back when you intervene and suggest the meeting be cut short for today. However, you would like to meet with your warring members of staff in 20 minutes and find out exactly what the problems are, who is causing them and what changes they can suggest to avoid a repetition of this crisis they are all now facing on the new product launch.

Plan how you will conduct this counselling interview. Remember to be yourself.

BRIEF FOR ADVERTISING EXECUTIVE

You are the advertising executive at Fast Foods International Ltd. The company started as a family business, supply sandwiches and buffet lunches to the local factory sites. They have expanded into the 'cook-chill' market and have until recently been supplying the local supermarkets. However, six months ago, you were hired by the sales and marketing manager to spearhead the market research and advertising for the development of new products for the national hypermarket chains.

You share an office with the project co-ordinator who has to ensure that purchasing of materials and components plus the production schedules coincide with the advertising launch. Both of you report to the sales and marketing manager and share a secretary to do your letters, filing and take messages. You often feel you don't actually share the secretary fairly; s/he seems to spend much more time dealing with purchasing difficulties.

Your are a graduate and a member of the Institute of Marketing and pride yourself on doing a good job. You secretly believe that you are the best qualified person there and don't have a very high opinion of those who have worked their way into a job. You were always taught that a tidy desk is the sign of a tidy mind and that chaos is bound to result otherwise. As a result, you have taken to tidying your colleague's desk after everyone has gone home in the evening because you can't bear to come in the next day and be faced with all that clutter. You have been expecting something to go wrong with this new 'No-Fat Hamburger' launch and you have been proved right in a project progress meeting with the whole department. Your two sales rep colleagues were enthusing about the prominent displays their retail customers have promised them and you have the advertising booked on national TV for the same week. However, the project co-ordinator has just announced that the vital, secret ingredient will not be available until a fortnight later than required and proceeds to blame your joint secretary.

You become angry and shout that it is not fair to blame the poor secretary; the project co-ordinator should consider their own workstyle first. You start to list all the things which have been annoying you such as the untidy desk, the papers left all over the place and the inconsiderate use of the telephone. In fact, you make it plain you were expecting something like this to happen and you have been proved right.

Your colleague is about to mount a defence, but your manager closes the meeting and asks both of you to come back in 20 minutes, prepared to discuss your respective differences and difficulties in sharing an office and to suggest some possible solutions.

Prepare for the counselling interview.

BRIEF FOR PROJECT CO-ORDINATOR

You are the project co-ordinator at Fast Foods International Ltd. It began as a small family firm which you joined straight from school. In those five years you have seen the company expand into the 'cook-chill' food market. Initially you were only supplying the local supermarkets but the new sales and marketing manager to whom you report has recently obtained a contract to supply a national hypermarket chain. This company growth means you have moved on from actually making the sandwiches and buffet lunches for the local factory sites and have taken on a much more office oriented job – anyone can handle the paperwork, can't they? You co-ordinate with the purchasing and production departments to ensure that a product is available at the time of an advertising launch.

You share an office with your colleague, the advertising executive, and you have a joint secretary who sits in the main office near the one desk and phone used by the two sales reps when they are in at different times. As you have been with the company since day one, you feel you have great knowledge about what goes on there and you certainly feel it gives you prior right to the secretary. After all, in the old days, everyone had to pull together and do whatever it took to resolve a crisis. Now your colleague, a graduate and a member of the Institute of Marketing, has arrived with all these academic theories. Well, what has that to do with reality?

When you look at your colleague's desk, there never seems to be anything much on it and the phone doesn't ring frantically all day either. To you this is an indicator that little or no work is going on in that area.

This morning you had to tell the weekly project progress meeting that the secret ingredient for the new 'No-Fat Hamburger' launch will be a fortnight late due to unexpected problems. The real problem is that you didn't make the application for Health Department approval in time but there is surely no need for the others to know that. So, you blame the secretary for not passing the information on to you sooner.

The two sales reps have already arranged for displays of the new product at their major retail sites and the advertising executive has a national TV campaign ready. Even so, you are surprised when you colleague starts to shout at you saying it is not fair to blame the secretary but that you should look at your own way of working. Your untidy desk and your loud telephone manner all come in for criticism so you decide to retaliate.

At that point your manager closes the meeting and asks to meet with the two of you in 20 minutes' time to discuss the apparent difficulties of working in close proximity to each other. Prepare for the interview.

20

Team player

Aim

To provide an opportunity to practise counselling skills. when working as a team.

Materials required

- Document 20.1 – Background (for everyone)
- Document 20.2 – Brief for managing director
- Document 20.3 – Brief for account executive
- Document 20.4 – Brief for producer
- Document 20.5 – Brief for director
- Document 20.6 – Brief for writer

Background

Building an effective team can be crucial for the effectiveness of a project or the general running of a department.

Method

Choose one of the four methods described in the Introduction and brief the participants accordingly, but note below.

This role play involves five roles: managing director, account executive, producer, director and writer.

The group size will affect timing and materials required. Adjust the method you use to suit. (Note: Method 4 – 'groups of 3' would become 'groups of 6'.)

Debriefing

1. Ask the participants in the role play for their reactions and feelings.
2. Open the discussion to the whole group noting points which arise on the flip chart.
3. If appropriate use the Belbin clarification (see additional guidance) to identify what is working well and what is going wrong in the team. It may even be useful for participants to identify the role they and the others adopted within the role play.
4. Use the counselling model to point out any problems.
5. Finish with a general discussion on working in teams.

Additional guidance

There are various team models, one of the best known being R. Meredith Belbin's *Management Teams* (Heinemann, 1981) which states that a fully effective team needs to have eight roles:

- The chairman
- The shaper
- The plant
- The monitor-evaluator
- The resource-investigator
- The company worker
- The team worker
- The finisher

You may want to make this role play part of a training session on Belbin.

BACKGROUND

Markwell Heine Productions specialize in producing corporate videos. They have grown from the MD and a friend working from a kitchen table to a company which employs 50 people. The company specializes in working for financial institutions and usually makes training programmes. One of their biggest clients is DD Investments which asks them to make four or five programmes a year. They are good clients, quite demanding and sometimes inflexible but generally willing to pay for good quality and original materials.

About six months ago you were given a contract to produce a programme on selling a new savings account. The team who worked on it were as follows:

- The account executive
- The producer
- The director
- The writer

The rest of the video crew were freelance and under the jurisdiction of the producer and director.

The account executive's role is to liaise between the client and the production team. They look after the project from the first idea through to the end. If there are any problems then they are to negotiate. If there are overruns on the budget or if the schedule has to be put back or brought forward, they approach the client. When there are serious problems they should contact the MD.

The producer is responsible for making sure that the production goes ahead: they will prepare a budget and a schedule, hire a video crew, arrange casting of actors, find a location, arrange editing and production of the final master tape.

The director is responsible for making the production work. They are in charge on the day, ensuring the programme looks and sounds right.

The writer has to take the client's brief and produce a script which will satisfy all their needs, including specific training and corporate messages.

BRIEF FOR MANAGING DIRECTOR

You are the managing director and chief executive of Markwell Heine Productions.

The programme on savings accounts for DD Investments was all quite straightforward and you did not even think about it. Until yesterday, that is.

Margaret Mays, their Head of Training, rang you up absolutely furious saying that they were not going to pay the final invoice and that they would not be giving your company any more work.

After she calmed down she explained:

1. The programme had a number of factual errors which means there will have to be a re-shoot.
2. The ideas and creativity in the programme were not as good as in previous programmes, although she was prepared to tolerate that if there had not been so many other problems.
3. The budget had increased twice from what she considered to be a very generous starting point. Each time she was told that a more creative idea had been found which would strengthen the programme enormously.
4. Damage was done to a branch office when filming took place, and nobody apologized or explained what had happened.
5. The manager of the branch complained about rudeness from the production team.
6. The project was not finished on time.

Her final comment was that the project had not been 'a team effort but just a number of people who happened to be working together'.

You decide you need to gather the team together and ask them what went wrong. You feel that it is the lack of teamwork which might be the cause of the problem.

Prepare for that meeting.

BRIEF FOR ACCOUNT EXECUTIVE

This is the first time you have worked with DD Investments. You are good at your job but felt at odds with the producer who had worked for the client many times before. Often the producer would not work through you but went direct to the client. This meant you were in the dark. So much so that when the MD phoned to say the client was not going to pay the final invoice and not use the company again you were amazed.

You found yourself doing some of the re-writing because the writer was working on two projects at the same time. You enjoyed this but were not always sure of the material. The writer was happy anyway.

Prepare for the meeting.

BRIEF FOR PRODUCER

You have worked on every DD Investments programme since they started coming to the company about four years ago. There is not much you do not know about them and their ways. You did not work well with the account executive during the last project. You felt that their role was to get the business in the first place, and then to let the professionals take over. There was no need for them to have any more than a monthly review on the programme. Yet the account executive wanted to be around all the time. It was a complete waste of time asking the account executive to tell the client something, when you could tell them equally well yourself. And of course they all knew you.

You were not very happy with the director. Recently they have been becoming restless. The director wants to have 'more ideas', as they call it. You think their work is slipping as a result. However, because you were there all the time, making sure the director did what you told them, there was no problem.

Prepare for the meeting.

BRIEF FOR DIRECTOR

You have worked for the producer twice before. Each time they wanted to do your job and not their own. There were many problems with the shoot. The crew became irritated by two people telling them to do different things and tempers got a little frayed. Some damage was done to the branch office which you pointed out to the account executive and the producer.

One of the other main problems was that you had plenty of ideas, which the producer agreed to at the time. It was only later that they said that they would increase the budget and by then it was too late to abandon them. This last project has made you think seriously about leaving and finding another job or going freelance.

You thought that the writer should have spent more time on the project. You were very critical of the account executive re-writing some amendments to the script. As they did not know the background to DD Investments you think they introduced some mistakes.

Prepare for the meeting.

BRIEF FOR WRITER

The trouble with this project was that you always seemed too busy. You were told by the producer to work on two projects at the same time, and also to check that the director was doing a good job.

You enjoyed helping the director but with the two projects it meant that you could not do all of the amendments the client requested. The account executive fancied themselves as a bit of a writer and so was happy to do the re-writes. They looked all right but afterwards you were a bit worried about a couple of points.

You spoke to the director but was told to keep quiet.

Prepare for the meeting.

21

The morning after

Aim

To practise listening and probing skills to discover the cause of the counsellee's problem.

Materials required

- Document 3.1 – Brief for manager
- Document 3.2 – Brief for employee

Background

The abuse of alcohol is serious. Often the problem may not be apparent: the drinking may not take place during work time and there may be no visible signs. However, symptoms such as persistent lateness can lead the manager to discover an alcohol problem. Not all heavy drinkers are alcoholics and not all alcoholics are heavy drinkers. It is not the quantity but the way it affects the employee which determines the severity of the problem. Therefore only when the problem is explored and discussed can the manager decide what, if any, action needs to be taken by the organization.

Alcoholics Anonymous is a voluntary self-help organization which does very good work in this area. It shows that alcoholism can affect anyone from the boardroom to the shop floor and of all ages or class. AA runs groups throughout the world (in the UK it can be found in Yellow Pages).

Method

Choose one of the four methods described in the Introduction and brief the participants accordingly.

Debriefing

1. Ask the participants in their role-playing groups to report their feelings.
2. Ask for comments from the whole group once each group has reported back.
3. Discuss the organization's policy on alcohol if there is one and the participants' personal views. Stress the need for understanding of what is a very common problem.

Additional guidance

Some participants may see alcoholism in simple terms: 'if they're drunk, there's a problem'. The reality is much more complicated, and an employee may function adequately while having a drink problem although the quality of the work is not as good as it could be.

BRIEF FOR MANAGER

One of your team has been late every day this week and you have to talk to them about it.

They have been a good worker and you have had no problems with them, though the last few months it seems as if they are not working quite as well as they have in the past.

You need to speak to them to find out if there is a reason why they have been late and try and talk about the problem. It may be appropriate to suggest possible solutions to the difficulty if you can, within any guidelines your organization may have.

Prepare for the interview.

BRIEF FOR EMPLOYEE

You have been late every day this week and you know there's going to be trouble at work!

The problem is that you've had a great deal on your mind. There always seems to be another bill around the corner, many of your friends have moved away, you find work quite stressful and it's difficult to relax these days. It's no wonder you have a drink after a heavy day. Now, however, it is happening more often than before and you never quite know when to stop. It wouldn't matter except the next day you feel bad and it's difficult to get up.

You have a drink problem but you do not want to admit it.

Prepare for the interview.

Tg

22

There's a good girl!

Aim

To improve understanding of sexism and sexist behaviour.

Materials required

- Document 22.1 – Brief for store manager
- Document 22.2 – Brief for Max Symes

Background

Equal opportunities has meant that in theory women are treated as equals. Although in UK law women now have a right to stand up against unacceptable behaviour, on a day-to-day basis sexism still flourishes.

It is very common for men to treat women in a way they would never treat another man – using pet names, flirting, touching etc. This is often thought of as being friendly or 'not meaning any harm'. Of course, in reality, it is not only annoying but unprofessional.

Method

Choose one of the four methods described in the Introduction and brief the participants accordingly.

Debriefing

1. Ask the store manager and then the department manager for their reactions and feelings.
2. Open the discussion to the whole group, noting points which arise on the flip chart.

BRIEF FOR STORE MANAGER

Max Symes has worked in the men's department of Hanwells since he was a boy, and now he's a few years away from retirement. He is friendly, well regarded by customers and staff and good at his job as department manager.

The problem is that he's what might have been called in his day 'a bit of a ladies' man'. He likes a pretty woman and is not averse to paying her a compliment. Unfortunately he does not realize the extent of what he is saying or doing. There have been a number of complaints over the last year and a serious one yesterday which has meant that you as the store manager have to act.

From the list, select three complaints to use in the role play with Max:

1. Repeatedly called one of the female assistants honey, love, darling, despite being asked by the woman not to.
2. Put his arm round a woman member of staff.
3. Insisted on kissing a woman assistant when she left for a holiday, even though they were not good friends.
4. Sent valentines to all the female staff.
5. Made a number of sexist jokes which upset one woman member of staff.
6. Embarrassed a woman who was leaving to get married with jokes about the honeymoon.
7. Asked one woman out for a drink after work, and when she refused brought in a bottle of wine instead.
8. Asked a senior woman manager why she was not married and made some sexist remarks. She was furious.

You have asked him to your office to discuss it. Prepare for the interview.

BRIEF FOR MAX SYMES

You have worked in the men's department of Hanwells since you were a boy, and now you are a few years away from retirement. You are friendly, well regarded by customers and staff and you believe you are quite good at your job as department manager.

You are not sure why the store manager wants to see you. There have been a few complaints about your behaviour and this sounds like another one. The trouble is that you have always had an eye for the girls and you cannot see what is wrong with paying them a compliment or making them feel special. However, you are happily married and there is no ulterior motive in your behaviour.

Yesterday a senior manager, a woman, came to your department. She started to tell you how to run things and, after all, everything has been running very well for the last 20 years. She was quite unfriendly, so you tried to humour her. You guessed she was not married and told her as a joke she would be happier if she had a good man there for entertainment! To your amazement she said it was sexual harassment and she was going to report it.

Prepare yourself for the interview with the store manager.

Tg

23

Working abroad

Aim

To help participants practise counselling an employee about to be transferred overseas.

Materials required

- Document 23.1 – Background (for counsellor and counsellee)
- Document 23.2 – Brief for manager
- Document 23.2 – Brief for Sam Lyons

Background

Sending an employee abroad is very stressful for all involved.

The organization has to invest money in resettling costs – training, shipping, accommodation, school fees, incentives, increased salaries and bonuses – and they cannot be sure that the manager who performs well in Milton Keynes will perform well in Milan or Milwaukee. It also has to replace the employee either on a temporary or a permanent basis and then re-incorporate the manager back in the UK operation. It is a calculated risk.

For the employee there is the fear of the unknown. Not only new staff, superiors and business but new culture, new geography and climate, perhaps a new language. In the past the manager has been able to cope with a change in job, and even a change in location within the UK because back at home there is The News (in English), take-away Chinese meals and a golf course or squash centre nearby. The same cannot be said of Taiwan, Turkey or Thailand.

Further, will this move be good for career improvement? Many employees see going abroad as a sideways step and often they are right to worry. They are not present when big decisions are made and so they may not appear as important to the organization as someone in London or Manchester.

For the employee's family there may be resentment and anger which the employee will have to deal with. The partner may not be able to work or if they can it may not be as rewarding or at as high a level. The Head of English in a comprehensive school, managing a staff of eight, may find themselves teaching English to children in private lessons. Home, family and friends have to be left behind and replaced with temporary accommodation, acquaintances and colleagues. This can put great strain on a relationship; old hands say that a posting overseas either makes or breaks it.

Of course it does not have to be a negative process. Some employees relish the opportunity to experience another culture, learn a new language and explore another country. Living conditions can be good in some countries and organizations may make the stay as comfortable as possible so that standards are almost luxurious. The experience gained can help back in the UK and can mean accelerated promotion. Preparation is the key. Employers and employees need to discuss the problems and try to plan for the smoothest of possible moves and tours abroad.

Method

Choose one of the four methods described in the Introduction and brief the participants accordingly.

Debriefing

1. Ask the counsellor and the counsellee to report back.
2. Ask for comments from the rest of the group.
3. Analyse those in terms of your counselling model.
4. Note these on a flip chart.
5. Follow up with any of the groups' own experiences and fears of working abroad.

Additional guidance

There are organizations which run orientation and familiarization courses on particular countries for employees being posted abroad. For example The School of Oriental and African Studies External Services run specialist courses on Japanese language and culture.

BACKGROUND

Job scales

	Grade	Salary (£)	Bonus (£)	Holiday (days)
Systems director	10	35,000	10,000	30
Senior manager	9	30,000	7,500	30
Dept manager	8	27,000	5,000	25
Section manager	7	25,000	5,000	25
Senior analyst/ programmer	6	23,000	–	20
Analyst/programmer	5	20,500	–	20
Analyst	4	19,000	–	20
Programmer	3	19,000	–	20
Senior admin	2	18,000	–	20
Admin	1	16,000	–	20

Job description

The banking business has three branches in Japan, Hong Kong and Singapore, the largest being Tokyo. They are run by local staff with one expatriate senior manager in each region. There are an average of six local staff in each region.

It has been decided that the automatic teller system (cash machines) operating in the UK and in Europe should be extended to the Far East. An experienced and motivated systems professional needs to set up a project team to analyse the problems of linking into the main system. The project is estimated to take up to two years. As a first step a new position will be created, based and living in Tokyo. This should be filled internally and, because this is a high-level profile, as quickly as possible.

The Far East – living conditions

Japan

Japan is a very large country consisting of four islands stretching north to south. Although Tokyo and the second city Osaka are vast urban sprawls there is a great deal of agriculture in open countryside. Travelling to these areas can be difficult, roads get blocked with traffic, and public transport is crowded and needs to be booked in advance. It can take three hours to reach a ski resort from Tokyo and then because of traffic 16 to get back!

Japanese is the language and out of the main cities it can be difficult to find anyone who can speak English; even in Tokyo communication can be a problem.

Japan has four distinct seasons, in the same way as the UK does, but in central Japan, in Tokyo, the winter is relatively mild but the summers hot and humid. There is great variation in Japan – the Southern Islands, Okinawa, are almost tropical and in the Northern Island, Hokkaido, snow lies most of the winter and there is good skiing.

Japanese culture on the surface seems to be similar to Western but this is misleading. At the same time as new Western ways have been absorbed by the Japanese, old traditions have still been maintained. Decisions are made on a group basis, and people from outside the group are often treated with suspicion. Middle-class women usually work at home and find it much harder than their Western counterparts to attain senior positions in business and there are complicated rituals and codes of conducts, about for example present giving, which can confuse and frustrate foreigners living there.

Property values and rents are some of the highest in the world. An average Japanese family will live either in a small three-room apartment in Tokyo or in a small four/five-room house in the suburbs with a commuting journey of up to two hours.

Hong Kong and Singapore

Hong Kong and Singapore are lively commercial cities with sophisticated business structures in place. The central area in both countries is heavily developed, but there are beaches and countryside not far out of the city centres.

Hong Kong and Singapore are two quite different countries. In Hong Kong Cantonese is the main language, but English is widely spoken. In Singapore many languages are spoken including Cantonese, Malay and Tamil, but English is also widely used.

Singapore is hot and humid year round, Hong Kong tends to have a similar climate to Singapore but is cooler in December and January.

Each country has its own separate identity although there is a strong Buddhist belief in Hong Kong and within the Chinese community in Singapore. Generally, though, Hong Kong and Singapore have a fairly Western-style society.

Terms and conditions

In addition to the normal salary and conditions the bank will also offer the following:

- Salary: 10 per cent of total salary will be paid into a UK bank account. A bonus of £5000 is awarded at the end of a successful two-year contract.

- Settling-in costs: there is a shipping and baggage allowance of 250kg, and a one-off payment of £2000.
- Education: the bank will cover costs of UK boarding school or International School in Tokyo.
- Accommodation: a furnished, Western-style two-bedroom apartment with sitting room, equipped kitchen and bathroom will be provided up to a monthly rent of £1200.
- Air fares: six return business-class flights during the two-year contract for the employee and partner will be granted. (Flights for dependent children will be negotiated separately.)
- Holidays: on renewal of the position after two years, there would be a three-week home visit allowance.
- Other: the bank will give a grant of £1000 for language training, and will pay for membership of one sports or social club.

BRIEF FOR MANAGER

You are the systems manager at a large bank. Your responsibility is to make sure that new computer systems are developed and implemented successfully. You have a team of ten including Sam Lyons. Sam is an excellent analyst/programmer (grade 5), able not only to research a problem and specify effectively but also to develop a sound program.

You have been asked to provide a systems manager (grade 7) for the branches you have in Japan, Hong Kong and Singapore. Sam would be ideal and has agreed in principle as this would mean promotion. You have both received a briefing pack from Personnel and you now need to discuss this career move. As this is an important job you have some flexibility to discuss the terms and conditions though obviously budget considerations apply and you must be careful not to set dangerous precedents.

Prepare for the meeting with Sam.

BRIEF FOR SAM LYONS

You are an analyst/programmer (grade 5) in a large bank. You work in a team of ten to research a problem and specify effectively and then develop a sound program. You have been asked to become a systems manager (grade 7) for the branches the bank has in Japan, Hong Kong and Singapore. You have agreed in principle but there are many aspects which worry you. You have received a briefing pack from Personnel and you now need to discuss this career move.

Background

You were born in 1958 and now live with your partner and have one child – Sophie (7). You have a three-bedroom cottage in a village with a large garden on a preferential bank mortgage, but you still have financial problems sometimes.

You have been with the bank since you left college; you enjoy the work and are quite ambitious. You family now live in Canada but you manage to see them every other year. Your partner is a buyer with a local department store and is in line to become senior buyer next year. They have always lived in that part of the country and their family lives nearby so they see them regularly.

Sophie goes to the local junior school which she likes. She is getting on well.

You are a keen squash player and belong to a local club. Your partner is fond of riding and you have just started learning.

You are worried about going to a managerial role without experience in the UK and wonder if that will be a problem you can do without when you are also trying to deal with a different culture and language.

Prepare for the meeting with your manager.

24

Working with HIV

Aim

To improve awareness of issues concerning HIV and AIDS.

Materials required

- Document 24.1 – Brief for manager
- Document 24.2 – Brief for employee

Background

AIDS stands for acquired immune deficiency syndrome. It is caused by the human immunodeficiency virus (HIV) which attacks the body's natural defence system and leaves it open to various infections and cancers.

Blood tests can detect these antibodies and a person with them is said to be HIV positive.

It is not known as yet how many people who are HIV positive will develop full-blown AIDS. The incubation period has greatly varied for those who do have AIDS. Most people who are HIV positive are well for most of the time but some develop minor symptoms such as swollen lymph glands, weight loss, sweats.

The HIV virus is transmitted most effectively by blood-to-blood contact (before screening through transfusions) and by drug users through sharing needles. Transmission through cuts and grazes is extremely unlikely. Accidential transmission in a laboratory or in the health care industry where blood products are used is possible, but safeguards and special guidelines should already exist to stop the spread of this and other diseases such as hepatitis. There have been no reported cases of infection from the administration of first aid, although first aiders should be given special guidance and reassurance if they are worried.

HIV is also transmitted through sex. Intercourse is the only sexual activity where transmission is proved. Other activities, as long as sperm is not passed, are extremely unlikely to pass on the virus. The use of condoms is the obvious way to stop the spread of the virus. Transmission through saliva has never been found.

The virus can also be passed from an infected mother to the unborn child.

Therefore HIV is not passed through casual, everyday contact. Kissing, hugging, touching, using the same cutlery or china, toilet seats, or swimming pools are not sources of transmission.

People with HIV infection will usually be able to work normally. Those who develop AIDS may suffer from severe illnesses which will affect performance. They should be treated in the same way as other employees with life-threatening illnesses.

AIDS can affect anyone so it should not be assumed that an infected employee has a particular sexual preference. Prejudice at this point can only do more harm.

Your organization may well have a policy on HIV and AIDS. However ACAS states that there is no reason to dismiss or discriminate against an employee with HIV or AIDS as there is no risk of transmission during normal working activities. It is against organizations giving in to pressure from other employees, stating that education and counselling is a better way of dealing with this problem. Similarly they believe that screening of existing or new staff is neither useful nor justified. There is no guarantee that someone who is found to be negative will remain so. To be HIV positive or to have AIDS does not necessarily mean that the job is done any less effectively.

Employees who go abroad should be advised of the particular dangers of unsterilized hospital equipment or unscreened blood and of casual sexual contacts.

ACAS recommend all organizations have an AIDS policy.

Method

Choose one of the four methods described in the Introduction and brief the participants accordingly.

Debriefing

1. Ask the counsellor and counsellee for their reactions and feelings.
2. Open the discussion to the whole group asking first of all for feeling about the role play and HIV and AIDS.
3. Ask for comments in relation to the counselling model.
4. Note any points on the flip chart.
5. Refer to the company's policy if there is one.

Additional guidance

This topic can arouse strong emotions. Keep to the facts and do not allow participants' fears and prejudices to corrupt that message.
Check whether your organization has a policy on HIV and AIDS.

BRIEF FOR MANAGER

You are a departmental manager. One of your staff, Paul Hanway, has been unusually quiet and low recently and when you tackled him about it, he has told you that he is HIV positive. He does not have AIDS. He feels relieved that you know and looks much better. You have reassured him that this does not need to affect his job status and that the organization will deal with him sympathetically. He will carry on working.

Unfortunately one of Paul's colleagues happened to notice some AIDS leaflets in his bag and has put two and two together and made five!

You have to see the colleague to discuss the situation.

BRIEF FOR EMPLOYEE

You work in the same department as Paul Hanway. Last week you noticed some AIDS leaflets in Paul's bag and as you think he might be gay you realize he has AIDS. You do not know a lot about this but are worried that he may be contagious.

You have decided to see the departmental manager to make him do something about Paul.

25

Working with MS

Aim

To improve skills in counselling an employee with multiple sclerosis.

Materials required

- Document 25.1 – Brief for counsellor
- Document 25.2 – Brief for counsellee

Background

In 1989 50,000 people in the UK suffered from multiple sclerosis. Most of those will have shown symptoms of the condition between the ages of 20 and 40.

A typical case is Jan. Aged 30, she noticed at first that she was easily tired, irritable and occasionally unsteady on her feet. Driving became difficult and long walks impossible. After many tests she was diagnosed as having MS.

The doctor explained that there was a great range of symptoms and progress. With luck there would be long periods of remission, but any sudden relapse could mean the illness was getting worse. MS is a chronic disease which cannot be cured by drugs or surgery.

Jan stayed well and relatively able to move around for seven years and then her legs became increasingly weak and powerless. She was unable to go out.

After that she became subject to muscle spasms, had urinary problems and was forced to use a wheelchair.

The illness can put a great strain on friends and family. A couple may find that the roles are reversed so that the partner who spent more time out of the home working now has to stay at home.

Stress can bring on a further deterioration. In Jan's case there was a seven-year period when she functioned effectively in her work; this must have been due to the support she received from colleagues and the organization she worked for.

The Multiple Sclerosis Society of Great Britain and Northern Ireland has almost 350 local branches which give support, practical advice, information on benefits, occasional financial help and provide special transport and day centres. Their address in the UK is:

25 Effie Road
Fulham SW6 1EE
Tel: 071 736 6267

Method

Choose one of the four methods described in the Introduction and brief the participants accordingly.

Debriefing

1. Ask for the reactions and feelings of the manager and the principal lecturer.
2. Take any comments from the other participants about how the role play went.
3. Analyse those comments with your counselling model.
4. Note areas of weakness on the flip chart.
5. The discussion can be opened out to other illnesses such as ME or repetitive strain injury. How would the group cope in those circumstances?

Additional guidance

Your organization may have a policy on MS, which should be incorporated.

Use the information in the background for a pre-role play training session on the main symptoms and stages of MS.

BRIEF FOR COUNSELLOR

You are head of a further education college. One of your members of staff, the principal lecturer in the hotel management department, has not been performing well. The lecturer worked for a large hotel chain before taking up a job about 10 years ago at the college as a junior lecturer. They have always worked well, despite the changes in the curriculum and the pressure of converting the existing diploma course to a degree course. They also lecture on hotel management, organize the selection procedure for students, and set and mark the yearly and final examinations as well as monitoring the ongoing assessment.

Out of work the lecturer is the head of the drama group in the college and produces two major works through the year, a musical and a play.

The lecturer is divorced and has no children.

The situation

You have noticed a decline in the lecturer's contribution in meetings and a listlessness and reluctance to take on extra work. Specifically they have forgotten to find a substitute for absences, have not handed in end of term marks for ongoing assessment on time and have refused to supervise a visit by a group to a local hotel because it was on their 'study day'.

Other staff have said the lecturer is uncharacteristically rude with them and an informal complaint has been made by the department's secretary.

It has come to a head because you have received the following anonymous letter.

> Dear sir/madam
> I thought you should know that the principal lecturer in the hotel management department has a severe drink problem and is probably an alcoholic. The lecturer in question turns up drunk to lectures and has fallen over on one occasion. I respect the individual's knowledge and experience but this drinking is interfering with my chances of getting a good grade on my degree.
>
> Something must be done or I will be forced to take the matter to a higher authority.
>
> Yours
>
> A student

Although you find anonymous letters distasteful you have to follow it up, and arrange to meet the lecturer.

Prepare for that encounter.

BRIEF FOR COUNSELLEE

You are the principle lecturer in the hotel management department of the college. You worked for a large hotel chain before taking up a job about 10 years ago at the college as a junior lecturer. You have always worked well, despite the changes in the curriculum and the pressure of converting the existing diploma course to a degree course. You lecture on hotel management, organize the selection procedure for students, and set and mark the yearly and final examinations as well as monitoring the ongoing assessment.

Out of work you are the head of the drama group in the college and produce two major works through the year, a musical and a play.

You are divorced and have no children.

The situation

About six months ago you started having health problems – you were easily tired, irritable and sometimes unsteady on your feet. Your doctor at first thought it was a trapped nerve, but then the condition worsened.

You had blurred vision which meant you had to stop driving, and caused you to fall over once in class. Your doctor arranged some tests and told you last week that you have multiple sclerosis.

Since then you have not known what to do, have not told anyone and have been walking around in a daze.

The head of the college has asked to see you, although you do not know why.

Prepare for that meeting.